ALAN HANKINSON

Coleridge Walks
the Fells

A Lakeland Journey Retraced

Fontana
An Imprint of HarperCollins*Publishers*

Fontana
An Imprint of HarperCollins*Publishers*,
77–85 Fulham Palace Road,
Hammersmith, London W6 8JB

Published by Fontana 1993
1 3 5 7 9 8 6 4 2

First published in Great Britain by
Ellenbank Press 1991

ISBN 0 00 637854 4

Set in Sabon

Printed in Great Britain by
HarperCollinsManufacturing Glasgow

To Joan

❧

'Now for our mountain sport.'
From *Cymbeline* by William Shakespeare

·

'And he went up into the mountain to pray, himself, alone.'
From the New Testament

·

'The farther I ascend from animated Nature, from men,
and cattle, and the common birds of the woods, and fields,
the greater becomes in me the Intensity of the feeling of Life.'
From *Collected Letters of S. T. Coleridge*

Contents

Foreword

by Melvyn Bragg

Entering into the spirit of this most enjoyable book, I began these notes on the top of Skiddaw, Good Friday 1991, a fine day without wind, misty clouds in the valleys, the peaks peering through the static steam-like clouds like remote tops in Japanese paintings. Skiddaw seemed uninhabited despite the holiday time of the year, no more than a dozen ramblers spotted from the time we joined the main mountain (we had come up from Dash Falls) until we left it. Two joggers bashing their feet and their brains in a pursuit which would have been thought pointless by Coleridge and is roundly despised by his contemporary chronicler, Alan Hankinson. People who go on to the fells, both of them would say, in order merely to pound up and down against a clock or a schedule miss everything the fells can bring you. I agree.

Like all good books, *Coleridge Walks the Fells* can be read on many different levels. If you want a plain *resumé* of the nine-day walk among the Western Fells which must be the first recorded great fell-walk and which includes the first recorded rock-climb – then here you have it. Alongside it you have the same journey ingeniously taken by Alan Hankinson about 200 years later in which he points out the similarities and differences en route. It is not all woe and loss by any means, which is one of several surprises.

Coleridge's account of his walk, which included the first love letter written on the top of Scafell, contains some of his most exuberant and vivid writing. Basically, he is charting his paths and his days but he is also attempting to discover and reflect accurately the relationship between the landscape and its effect on his mind, the exertion and the impact on his body and his thoughts, the truth of a man in nature. One description – of his descent from Scafell – still trembles off the page and is unsurpassed, in my experience, by anything I have encountered

on the subject of someone faced with the danger and ines-
capability of a route on the rocks.

Hankinson's book is constructed like the best day's
walking: you have a destination and a route in mind but should
anything take your eye or your fancy along the way then you
must have the time and the sense to explore it. So Hankinson
ambles off into literary thumbnail sketches, sniffs around local
history, points out the more dramatic changes along the way
and describes his own intrepid explorations into various public
houses. We meet a casualty (not fatal) in Wasdale which takes
us into a brief history of Hankinson's heroes, the professional
intellectual men who came to the Western Fells in the last
quarter of the last century combining hard thinking with hard
climbing. A sopping wet visit to the Fish Hotel in Buttermere
triggers the story of Mary Robinson and the impostor, Hatfield.
And so the book zigzags between Coleridge and the present,
one writer and another, the effect being of two minds focused
on the same subject, bringing entertaining and intriguing contrasts. At one stage, there is a comparison between Rousseau
and Coleridge on the subject of the connection between walking
and thinking: Hankinson himself is clearly one of the walker-
thinkers of the world.

Coleridge was one of the great minds of English literature.
It is a most fortunate circumstance that he came to this part of
the world while still at the height of his immense powers and
wrote so well, in some ways so supremely well about it. Alan
Hankinson wisely restricts himself to the nine days – after doing
us the courtesy of opening pages which give us the period and
its context. In these nine days Coleridge discovered the fells in
a way never recorded before and never matched since. In this
book we follow in his footsteps and we see inside his mind. It
is a considerable feat and a rare treat.

Acknowledgements

For nearly 20 years I have wanted to write a book about the years when Coleridge lived in Keswick. The problem was to find anyone who wanted to publish it. This was solved when two friends, Kelly Davis and Ian Francis, decided to branch out into publishing and thought they would like to include this book in their first list. I am grateful to both of them for much help and encouragement, and especially to Kelly for her meticulous and expert editing of my typescript.

Many people helped me as I followed Coleridge's footsteps around the Lake District, and they are acknowledged in the book.

I have to thank Oxford University Press for permission to quote from their *Collected Letters of Samuel Taylor Coleridge*, and Princeton University Press, New Jersey, for permission to quote from their *Notebooks of Samuel Taylor Coleridge*, and Irvine Hunt for permission to quote from the works of Norman Nicholson.

The Staff of the Photographic Service of the British Library kindly sent me photographs of the appropriate *Notebook*. I also received help with photographs from Mr George Holt of Keswick.

Mary Gay Pearson of Keswick drew the map of Coleridge's route.

I am indebted to several people for information: to Mrs Susan Johnson for information about her father, the Rev. H. H. Symonds; to Mrs Muriel Files for information about A. P. Rossiter and the early ascents of Broad Stand; to Miss Sheila Huftel for advice about Coleridge's character; and to Dr William Rollinson for sharing with me, as he always does, his great knowledge of Lake District history.

Dr Michael Cox of Caldbeck helped me with medical information. Mr James Francis of Lorton is the young man who kindly met me on top of Scafell with his climbing rope.

It was good of Melvyn Bragg, who is a busy man, to find time to write a foreword. Mr George Bott of Keswick scrutinised the typescript for me, pointed out the howlers and made many valuable suggestions. Finally, my deepest thanks of all to Joan Wilson – to whom the book is dedicated – for taking some of the photographs, checking each chapter as it was finished, making many corrections, offering fresh ideas and helping me in ways too numerous to mention.

A Note About the Text

There are many quotations in this book from Coleridge's letters and notebook jottings. With very few exceptions, they are printed here exactly as he wrote them – with occasional misspellings, his haphazard scattering of capital letters, his sometimes eccentric punctuation. Once or twice, to try to make his meaning more easily apparent, I have inserted a comma or a dash. Within the quoted passages I have used square brackets to give the meaning of dialect words that he used.

List of Illustrations

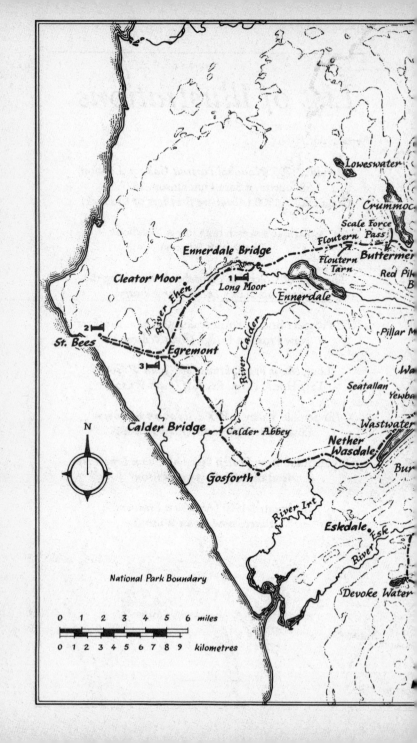

Loweswater

Crummoc

Scale Force

Floutern Pass

Buttermer

Floutern Tarn

Red Pik

B

Ennerdale Bridge

1

Long Moor

Ennerdale

Cleator Moor

River Ehen

Pillar M

2

St. Bees

Egremont

3

River Calder

Wa

Seatallan

Yewba

Wastwater

Calder Bridge

Calder Abbey

Nether
Wasdale

Bur

Gosforth

N

River Irt

Eskdale

River Esk

National Park Boundary

Devoke Water

0 1 2 3 4 5 6 miles

0 1 2 3 4 5 6 7 8 9 kilometres

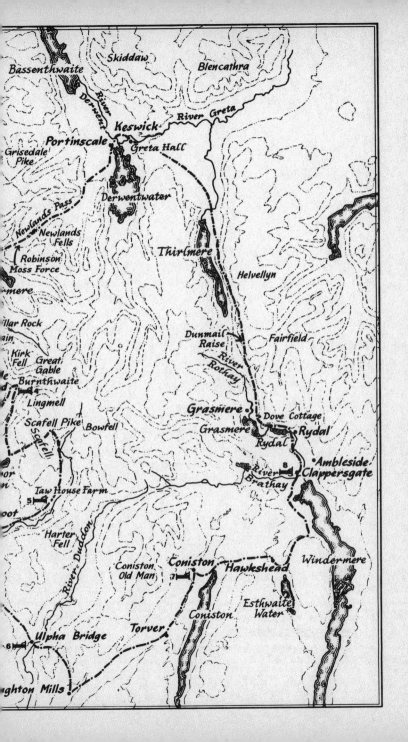

CHAPTER ONE

Setting the Scene

Shortly after midday on Sunday 1st August 1802, Samuel Taylor Coleridge strode down the hill from Greta Hall, his Keswick home, a knapsack over one shoulder and a broom-handle for a walking-stick, at the start of a nine-day walk around the Lake District.

On Sunday 13th August 1989 – 187 years and 12 days later – I set off from the same spot to follow, as closely as possible, in his footsteps. Like Coleridge, I walked alone. Like him, I did not book accommodation ahead but advanced hopefully, trusting that I would find somewhere to lay my head each evening. I tried to do the journey in his daily stages, and succeeded – up to a point.

The 'footsteps' form has become a popular one with writers. In the summer of 1964 Richard Holmes (now more than halfway through a fine biography of Coleridge) followed the route through the Cevennes that Robert Louis Stevenson had walked, with his recalcitrant donkey, 86 years before. Bernard Levin traced Hannibal's path across southern France and over the Alps to produce a book and a television series made memorable by his 'Big White Carstairs' tropical shorts. Others, for various motives, have tracked the evangelising journeys of St Paul, the road to Canterbury that Chaucer's pilgrims took, the trail that John Muir blazed across the Sierra Nevada of California. At least two writers – Geoffrey Moorhouse and Beryl Bainbridge – have toured the places that J. B. Priestley visited on his *English Journey*, published in 1934, to update his report on the state of the nation.

My aim was different from any of theirs. The idea was to look out for all the things that Coleridge noted on his walk that are still to be seen, virtually unchanged; also the things he saw which are no longer there, and the things that are there now but were not when he passed by; and, in this way, to try to form some picture of what has happened to this unique corner of England in the intervening years. So this is an account of three journeys: the one that Coleridge made, which was an exploration and an escape; the one I made, which was more of an investigation; and the long, complex journey that the Lake District has made in almost two centuries.

Luckily, much is known about Coleridge's walk. He carried a small notebook and stopped frequently to jot down, while they were still fresh in his mind, all his observations and adventures, the feelings they inspired, the responses they aroused in that teeming and tireless mind. He then used these notes to form the basis of long, vivid and more literary letters that he wrote to the woman he had fallen guiltily in love with, Sara Hutchinson. These primary sources have survived almost intact and, thanks to assiduous modern scholarship – much of it North-American – they are available in published form.

Coleridge, who enjoyed coining new words, called his walk a 'circumcursion'. He ended where he started. His route followed a wavering but roughly circular course, anti-clockwise in direction, well over 100 miles in distance, involving the ascent and descent of more than 10,000 vertical feet, often on steep and stony ground. He saw all the higher mountains of the Lake District and most of its lakes and valleys, though he missed out Ullswater and Hawes Water and the eastern fells. He passed through three counties, for at that time – and for a further 170 years, until Prime Minister Edward Heath had the county boundaries redrawn – Keswick was in Cumberland, Coniston was in North Lancashire, Rydal and Grasmere were in Westmorland. He touched the shore of the Irish Sea at St Bees. He rested and wrote part of a letter on the summit of Scafell, the second highest point of land in England. Descending from there, he took a short cut that involved him in the first recorded rock-climb ever made in this country.

It is hard, nowadays, to appreciate the sheer boldness of his undertaking. It was a journey without precedent. No one before him, and no one but Coleridge in his time, dreamt of walking over and among the high fells, alone, in all weathers, getting off the shepherds' tracks, for the sheer fun of it. Mountains were still seen as dangerous and repellent places, treacherous and profitless. Even William Wordsworth, a Lake District man by birth and upbringing and a powerful pedestrian, hired a local guide when he wanted to go to the summit of Scafell Pike.

Coleridge's achievement is all the more remarkable in the light of his condition and circumstances. These could hardly have been more discouraging.

He was nearly 30 years old and had long suffered from a variety of physical complaints, most notably rheumatism. To suppress the pain he had been taking ever-increasing doses of laudanum, a tincture of opium and alcohol. By 1802, according to most accounts, he was addicted.

He was a married man with two young sons and a third child on the way. But the marriage was in trouble. His love for Sara Hutchinson, at odds with his strong belief in the sanctity of Christian marriage, tormented him with guilt. The household, which was sometimes awakened in the middle of the night by his drug-induced nightmare screams, was often shattered during the day by fierce connubial shouting matches. In addition, the power of poetic creation, which he prized above all else, seemed to have deserted him. And this at a time when Wordsworth was writing more prolifically and more powerfully than ever. His long walk gave Coleridge an escape from all these problems and pressures.

The urge to escape has rarely been given the recognition it deserves as a motivating force among those who go off on adventurous expeditions. When they come to write it up afterwards, as they frequently do, these people – explorers, mountaineers, lone navigators – tend to play that aspect down, presumably because they do not want to further upset the loved ones left behind at home. So we read much about the call of the wilderness, the spirit of adventure and man's instinct to explore. But man's instinct to escape is also powerful, and has been intensified perhaps by the crowded conditions, rigid routines and nagging anxieties of modern life. It was the relatively new urban, industrialised society in Britain and Germany in the mid-nineteenth century that produced the adventure sports –

mountaineering and rock-climbing, pot-holing and small boat sailing. The idea of breaking out and 'getting away from it all' is perennially attractive. Nothing is more liberating and enlivening – for a while.

Coleridge had always been a natural escaper. As a child he escaped into books and solitary reveries. When he ran into trouble at Cambridge he bolted to enlist as a trooper in a cavalry regiment. As a husband, even in the first happy years of the marriage, he was rarely at home at times of crisis. He could always find reasons for his derelictions, but the pattern was repeated too often for them to carry conviction.

In the summer of 1802 he certainly had much to want to escape from, and for the nine days of his walk he escaped completely. He was never many miles from home but he was, in effect, in a different world. The delight, the exultation of this, shines through his writing. It made a marvellous break for him, stimulating and fascinating and exciting, perhaps the last time in his life when the whole of his being – mind and body, heart and soul and will – were working harmoniously and vigorously together, at full stretch.

The Time

In the summer of 1802 Britain was enjoying a respite in its long war against revolutionary France. The Peace of Amiens, signed in March, had ended more than nine years of intermittent fighting, though few supposed that the peace would last. King George III, in one of his periods of sanity, had called it 'the experimental peace'. But everyone welcomed the break. The war had so far brought little glory to British arms and had laid heavy burdens on the nation's economy. Prime Minister Pitt ('the Younger') had run the national debt up to unprecedented heights. For the first time in British history there was a tax on personal incomes.

The government, terrified that French ideas of republicanism and social justice and democracy might infect the British people and undermine the structure of society, had enacted a series of draconian measures to suppress any move towards radicalism or 'treason'. The mood grew more hysterical when it looked as if the French might invade. In the late summer of 1797 – when Coleridge and Wordsworth and his sister Dorothy were enjoying their new-found friendship and roaming the Quantock hills at all hours of the day and night, talking politics and philosophy and planning to change the course and character of English poetry – some of the locals thought their behaviour so suspicious that reports were sent to the Home Secretary in London and he despatched an experienced agent, John Walsh, to keep them under surveillance. At first he thought they were French spies, prospecting for likely landing places. Soon, though, he decided they were merely 'a mischievous gang of disaffected Englishmen'.

Walsh was a few years behind the times. Coleridge and Wordsworth had both been enthusiastic supporters of the French Revolution in its first heady years. In the summer of 1790 Wordsworth and a college friend from Cambridge had walked across France from north to south at the very time when the country was celebrating the first anniversary of the Fall of the Bastille. The following year he returned to France for a longer visit, which he later recalled in the famous lines from 'The Prelude':

> ... Bliss was it in that dawn to be alive,
> But to be young was very Heaven!

Coleridge, too, was swept along by the reformist tide, openly preaching the cause at Cambridge and then in the Bristol area. But the excesses of 'The Terror', the fratricidal infighting among the revolutionary factions in Paris, then the blatant imperialism of the revolutionary armies and the emergence of a new tyrant, Napoleon Bonaparte, First Consul for Life – all these brought disillusionment. By the turn of the century neither Wordsworth nor Coleridge was pro-French.

In the event the Peace of Amiens lasted just over 12 months. Many leading members of English society took the chance to cross the Channel to see how Paris had changed, appraise the new fashions, and to catch sight, if possible, of Napoleon himself. Wordsworth, in a fierce sonnet, denounced these sightseers as 'men of prostrate mind'. He could take the puritanical high-sounding line on occasion, and did so more and more as he grew older. But, as it happens, he and his sister Dorothy were in France that summer, not for frivolous, touristic reasons but on serious and intensely private business – business that is revealing about Wordsworth's character and also about the nature of his relationship with Coleridge.

He and Dorothy went to Calais to see Annette Vallon and her daughter Caroline. Wordsworth had met Annette in Orléans 11 years before, when he was an ardent 21-year-old and she a charming young Frenchwoman. They fell in love, made love and, in December 1792, a daughter, Caroline, was born. By that time Wordsworth was in Paris, on his way back to England. Soon after, Britain and France were at war and the lovers were separated for many years. Occasional letters in each direction got through, but by the time the Peace of Amiens was signed Wordsworth was engaged to marry a childhood friend, Mary Hutchinson, elder sister of the Sara Hutchinson whom Coleridge loved. The wedding was fixed for early October 1802. Wordsworth took the chance offered by the temporary peace to arrange a visit to Calais where he might explain matters to Annette and see his daughter Caroline.

It was the honourable thing to do. But Wordsworth was a Cumberland man born and bred, and, though not of peasant or farming stock, he had much of the close, careful, canny approach to life that is associated with the breed. He could be close-lipped and secretive. In 'The Prelude', although there are many pages about his youthful visits to France and his revolutionary fervour at that time, there is no hint of an affair with Annette. No one outside his immediate family was ever told about it. And they kept the secret so faithfully that the story of Annette and Caroline and their relationship with the father of English Romantic poetry did not become public knowledge until the 1920s and then as the result of French, not English, research.

Wordsworth did not even tell his closest friend, as is made clear by a passing remark in a letter Coleridge wrote to Sara Hutchinson the day after he got home from his 'circumcursion', the only reference in any of his letters to the affair:

> Dear little Caroline! – Will she be a ward for Annette? –
> Was the subject too delicate for a Letter? – I suppose
> so.

Coleridge knew the purpose of the trip to Calais was 'delicate'. He knew the names of Annette and Caroline but was unsure of their relationship. Nor did he know where Wordsworth fitted into the picture. Coleridge was a man of strong affections and also one of great curiosity, and it is impossible to believe that he could have refrained from asking the relevant questions. There was no lack of opportunity. Before starting on the journey to France, William and Dorothy spent three days as Coleridge's guests at Greta Hall, and when they set off he walked with them for 7 miles or so. 'He was not well,' Dorothy noted in her *Journal*, 'and we had a melancholy parting after having sate together in silence by the road-side.' One can only assume that Coleridge had asked Wordsworth earlier on about the reasons for the journey, and that his inquiries had been rebuffed or firmly evaded. It is a measure of the enormous respect Coleridge had for his friend that he was able to hold his tongue during those last long moments before they went their separate ways.

They were still close friends, though poles apart in temperament. Coleridge was impulsive, extrovert and confessional, always reaching out for human contact, ready to share almost everything about himself with others. His letters and conversations often took the form of outpourings – his hopes and plans, his self-doubts and self-disgust, the state of his mind and heart, the state of his marriage, the state of his bowels – all this, and much else, was discussed and described, in great and sometimes shocking detail. Wordsworth could hardly have been more different. He was an austere, taciturn, undemonstrative man. He felt deeply but it was only to his sister and later to his wife, and then not very often, that he would open his heart. The passion was kept for the poetry and even there it was firmly controlled; 'emotion recollected in tranquillity', in his famous phrase.

The Annette affair shows the way their relationship was changing. In the first days of their friendship, five years before,

Coleridge was the leading partner. Though two and a half years younger, he was already something of a public figure, while Wordsworth was still unknown to the world. But it was the fecundity and generosity of Coleridge's mind, his brilliance and ebullience that made him *primus inter pares*. The ideas he expounded at that time had great influence on Wordsworth's thinking. By 1802, however, the positions had been reversed. Wordsworth's was always the stronger character – steadier, more resolute and more calculating. He had an inner certainty that his friend could only admire and envy. His was the stronger position, too; happy in his sister's loyal companionship, looking forward to his marriage, writing more and better than ever, quite sure now that he had been right to risk everything to follow his poetic star. 'He is a great, a true Poet,' Coleridge wrote to a friend, 'I am only a kind of Metaphysician.'

The Wordsworths set off for Calais in mid-July. They called on friends en route, and made a leisurely progress, so that they landed in France on the very day that Coleridge began his big walk. Perhaps their absence was another way in which his walk gave him an escape from his normal life, though William and Dorothy were rarely far from his thoughts.

The war with France had been the chief national concern in the previous decade, but there were other and more fundamental forces at work which made this a period of faster social change than the country had ever experienced. The population was increasing. In 1750 the population of England had been reckoned at about six million; by 1801, the year of the first census, it had risen by 50 per cent. And it was a population on the move. The harnessing of steam power had launched an industrial revolution which, in its turn, created a social revolution. Mills and factories sprang up and around them, in South Lancashire and Yorkshire and the Midlands and elsewhere, close-packed rows of terraced houses were built for the workers. People poured into these new centres, eager for regular work, driven from the countryside by the decline in cottage industry.

The eighteenth century had seen something of an agricultural revolution too, as men brought new scientific knowledge to bear on age-old problems of husbandry. Common land was enclosed and hedgerows planted to mark the boundaries of the new farms. As usually happens in times of economic change, those who were firmly founded when it began did well out of it; those who were not, did not. But these developments scarcely touched the farmers of the Lake District, whose methods of work with the mountain sheep and the valley pastures remained the same as they had been for many centuries.

The Place

In his *Guide through the District of the Lakes,* first published in 1810, Wordsworth regretted the changes that had been taking place in the region and gave a somewhat idealised description of the hill farmer's life as he believed it had been lived for many centuries until around 1750:

> Towards the head of these Dales was found a perfect Republic of Shepherds and Agriculturalists, among whom the plough of each man was confined to the maintenance of his own family, or to the occasional accommodation of his neighbour. Two or three cows furnished each family with milk and cheese. The chapel was the only edifice that presided over these dwellings, the supreme head of this pure Commonwealth; the members of which existed in the midst of a powerful empire, like an ideal society or an organised community, whose constitution had been imposed and regulated by the mountains which protected it. Neither high-born nobleman, knight nor esquire, was here; but many of these humble sons of the hills had a consciousness that the land, which they walked over and tilled, had for more than five hundred years been possessed by men of their name and blood ....

The picture probably owes less to historical evidence than it does to Wordsworth's central conviction that there is something character-forming, ennobling even, about hard labour in a harsh but free environment. Even so, there is something in what he says. Until the mid-eighteenth century the Lake District had been a remote and little-known region, more than content to be generally ignored. Its farms were worked by sturdy folk who took pride in their independence and in the continuity of their family holdings.

Wordsworth goes on to bewail the fact that this 'ideal society' had been invaded and disturbed by wealthy outsiders, eager to acquire prime lakeside sites and disfigure them with obtrusive houses and 'improvements' to the landscape which involved felling native trees and replacing them with alien conifers:

> The lakes had now become celebrated; visitors flocked hither from all parts of England; the fancies of some were smitten so deeply, that they became settlers; and the Islands of Derwentwater and Winandermere [Windermere], as they offered the strongest temptation, were the first places seized upon, and were instantly defaced by the intrusion.

Having been ignored throughout the ages, the Lake District found itself becoming, in the closing decades of the eighteenth century, increasingly popular. It was not only the wealthy coming to build themselves holiday homes; tourists were also pouring in for sightseeing holidays. A few days after he settled his family into Greta Hall in July 1800, Coleridge wrote to a friend:

> It is no small advantage here that for two thirds of the year we are in complete retirement – the other third is alive and swarms with Tourists of all shapes and sizes and characters – it is the very place I would recommend to a novellist or farce writer.

By the turn of the century the tourist industry, which has since become the mainstay of the District's economy, was firmly established.

It was not the first industry to flourish there. In prehistoric times, 2,000 years BC and more, there was a major manufacturing and exporting business, quarrying the fine-grained volcanic rock in the high central fells and making axe heads. The Vikings, who arrived in the ninth century AD, grazed their sheep in the mountains and established a thriving wool trade. They and their successors, the great monastic land-owners of medieval times, branched out into subsidiary cottage industries – cleaning, spinning and weaving the wool. In the valleys the abundant water power fuelled many mills: grinding corn; processing wool, cotton and linen; turning wood. There had been mining in the Middle Ages and this increased dramatically in the second half of the sixteenth century when extensive seams of copper, lead, black lead and other valuable minerals were discovered in the fells. The broadleaf forests that covered the hillsides up to the 2,000-foot contour were cut down to produce charcoal to smelt the ores. It was perhaps providential that, as the seams were finally worked out and as increasing mechanisation destroyed the old cottage industries, the Lake District found a new role, as a holiday resort.

Until the middle of the eighteenth century it did not occur to anyone to visit the Lake District for pleasure. On the contrary, it was a place to be avoided. Daniel Defoe, a sharp-eyed reporter, spoke for many when he described the area in his *Tour through the whole Island of Great Britain*:

> ... Nor were these hills high and formidable only, but they had a kind of unhospitable terror in them. Here were no rich pleasant valleys between them ... but all barren and wild, of no use or advantage either to man or beast .... Here we entered Westmorland, a country eminent only for being the wildest, most barren and frightful of any that I have passed over in England, or even in Wales it self; the west side, which borders on Cumberland, is indeed bounded by a chain of almost unpassable mountains, which, in the language of the country, are called Fells ....

Fifty years later, in 1773, Dr Johnson and James Boswell made their famous journey to the Hebrides and the Doctor's response to mountain landscape was much the same as Defoe's:

> An eye accustomed to flowering pastures and waving harvests is astonished and repelled by this wide ex-

tent of hopeless sterility. The appearance is that of matter incapable of form or usefulness, dismissed by nature from her care, left in its original state, or quickened only with the sullen power of useless vegetation.

When Boswell tried to get him to concede that one mountain was 'immense', he would not even allow that: 'No; it is no more than a considerable protuberance.'

In Britain attitudes began to change in the mid-eighteenth century. Two painters, William Bellers and then Thomas Smith of Derby, went to Keswick. Bellers produced scenes of pastoral serenity and delight. Smith, in contrast, exaggerated all he saw to convey a sense of drama and danger, full of storm clouds and massive crags. For many people the published prints of their pictures gave the first hint that such strange and wonderful scenes could be found in England.

Soon after the painters came the writers. Among the earliest was the Reverend Dr John Brown, who had grown up at Wigton, within sight of the northern fells. He wrote an ecstatic account of Derwentwater in a letter to a friend and this was published in 1766, then reprinted many times under the title 'A Description of the Lake at Keswick'. He summed up his excited impressions thus:

> ... the full perfection of KESWICK consists of three circumstances, *Beauty, Horror* and *Immensity* united ... to give you a complete idea of these three perfections, as they are joined in KESWICK, would require the united powers of *Claude, Salvator* and *Poussin*. The first should throw his delicate sunshine over the cultivated vales, the scattered cots, the groves, the lake, and wooded islands. The second should dash out the horror of the rugged cliffs, the steeps, the hanging woods, the foaming waterfalls; while the grand pencil of *Poussin* should crown the whole with the majesty of the impending mountains.... I walk forth in this stupendous scene, as into the grandest earthly temple of the Creator.

In this passage Brown managed to embrace all the qualities that attracted the first tourists: the Arcadian charm of the lakeside scene; the enjoyable frisson of horror aroused by the towering cliffs; the sense of sublimity and religious awe inspired by the presiding mountain tops; and what soon came to be known as 'the picturesque', the resemblances of Lake District scenes to the paintings of many popular artists – nature imitating art.

The leading poet of the period, Thomas Gray, read Brown's description and, in October 1769, went to see for himself. He kept a full journal which was published six years later, and it was this – above all else – that stimulated public interest in the Lake District.

Gray had an observant eye and a lovely prose style, cool and limpid and lyrical. Approaching Keswick from the East, he halted his carriage and, in his own words, 'saw from an eminence, at two miles distance, the Vale of Elysium in all its verdure, the sun then playing on the bosom of the lake, and lighting up all the mountains with its lustre'.

Gray spent more than a week in the region, exploring every day. He was not above the 'picturesque' impulse. By his own admission, he made frequent use of a Claude glass, a small convex mirror which you held up, your back to the view, in order to compose and frame the perfect landscape. On the whole his account is sensible as well as sensitive, but he sometimes fell willing victim to the eighteenth-century penchant for 'Gothick' excesses. He went up Borrowdale as far as Grange and – despite the fact that there was a centuries-old packhorse route up the valley and over the passes beyond Seathwaite – reported: '... all farther access is here barr'd to prying Mortals'. And in Borrowdale itself, where the valley closes in below Gowder Crag, he quickened his step and did not speak, lest the 'agitation of the air' should provoke a rock avalanche from the 'impending' crags on either side.

Clearly the practice of filling the visitors' heads with nonsense is as old as the tourist trade itself. A few years after Gray's visit one of the Keswick guides, Thomas Hutton, was said to conduct his clients to the summit of Skiddaw and successfully persuade them that they could see the North Sea – a physical impossibility. He also told them that in winter at the head of Borrowdale the wind sometimes blew so ferociously that fully grown ewes would be swept high into the air, swirled around and dashed to their deaths against the crags.

By 1778 the *Monthly Magazine* was able to proclaim that 'to make the *Tour* of the Lakes, to speak in fashionable terms, is the *ton* of the present hour'. The arrival of the 'curious visitors', usually in carriages and in annually increasing numbers, was immediately exploited. Such hotels as there were smartened themselves up; before long there were two rival museums in Keswick; guidebooks appeared and maps of the lakes, indicating the best viewpoints; brass cannon were installed to impress visitors with the reverberations of the echoes from surrounding cliffs; there were annual regattas on Bassenthwaite Lake and Derwentwater, with rowing races and mock sea battles and firework displays at night. Many of the more active locals supplemented their incomes by taking the visitors fishing or guiding them about the valleys and the fells.

Some took their passion for the picturesque to ludicrous extremes. William Gilpin, a headmaster and an amateur artist, laid down rigid rules governing the proper appreciation of wilderness landscape and its translation on to canvas. If the scene before you seemed inadequate, he said, you had not just the right, but the positive duty to improve it in your picture. Of the ascent of Dunmail Raise from Grasmere, he wrote:

> The whole view is entirely of the horrid kind. Not a tree appeared to add the least cheerfulness to it. With regard to the adorning of such a scene with figures, nothing could suit it better than a group of banditti. Of all the scenes I ever saw, this was the most adapted to the perpetration of some dreadful deed.

Naturally enough, this sort of thing was quickly subjected to ridicule. James Plumptre wrote a comic opera, *The Lakers*, deriding the excesses of the picturesque travellers. William Combe's long narrative, in rhyming couplets, *Tour of Dr Syntax in Search of the Picturesque*, was brilliantly illustrated by Thomas Rowlandson. The group that came to be known, misleadingly, as 'the Lake poets' – Wordsworth, Robert Southey and Coleridge himself – regarded the 'picturesque' tourists with amused contempt and the rich builders of holiday homes with anger.

Coleridge wrote of 'yonder sallow-faced and yawning Tourist' and noted: 'Gold-headed Cane on a pikteresk Toor . . .'. He was outraged by the obtrusive new houses going up at the head of Windermere:

> Mr Law's White palace – a bitch! . . . .
> The damned Scoundrel on the right hand with his house and a Barn built to represent a Chapel – His Name is Partridge from London – and 'tis his Brother's Cow-pen. This *Fowl* is a stocking-weaver by Trade – have mercy on his five wits!

And he was amused to see 'Ladies reading Gilpin's etc. while passing by the very places instead of looking at the places'.

Much the same observation had been made a few years earlier by a man who was perhaps Coleridge's most important predecessor, Captain Joseph Budworth. In his book *A Fortnight's Ramble to the Lakes* he recorded the description his guide had given him of a client he was rowing across Windermere who exclaimed:

> 'Good God! how delightful! how charming! I could live here for ever! Row on, row on, row on, row on,' and after passing one hour of exclamations upon the Lake, and half an hour at Ambleside, he ordered his horses into his phaeton, and flew off to take (I doubt not) an equally-flying view of Derwentwater.

Budworth was a retired army captain who had lost an arm at the siege of Gibraltar but retained a robust spirit, an appetite for prodigious meals and a keen eye for pretty girls. In the summer of 1792 he visited the Lake District, covered more than 240 miles in two weeks and – unlike the great majority of the visitors, who rarely ventured more than a few yards from their carriages – hired guides to escort him up the fells. He described it all in his book which is refreshingly bluff and entirely free of attitudinising. Budworth climbed to the summit of Skiddaw and was probably the first tourist to ascend Helm Crag above Grasmere. He got up at 4 one morning to traverse Fairfield and Helvellyn and was back in the valley before 11 a.m. to tackle a breakfast of mutton, ham, eggs, buttermilk, whey, tea, bread and butter and cheese, at 7 pence a head. Just below the top of the Langdale Pikes he was so unnerved by the steepness of the slope that he bound up his right eye so he could not see the drop, then edged his way along a narrow sheep track, holding one end of his guide's fell pole to steady himself. He did not have Coleridge's head for heights and he lacked something of Coleridge's boldness. But the exhilaration he experienced was very like that which Coleridge was to find a few years later:

> The air upon the mountains is so clear, I fancied myself as brisk as the sheep around me; and the hilarity I enjoyed was such as I have felt after drinking champaigne, with the difference of a longer continuance without the relaxation it occasions. A certain gaiety pervades me at the recollection, and I trust it will pleasure my fancy whenever it bursts upon my memory.

The Man

Coleridge was interested in almost everything, in himself most of all. In a letter dated November 1796 he offered an unflattering but substantially accurate self-portrait:

> As to me, my face, unless when animated by immediate eloquence, expresses great Sloth, and great, indeed almost ideotic, good nature. 'Tis a mere carcase of a face; fat, flabby, and expressive chiefly of inexpression. – Yet I am told that my eyes, eyebrows, and forehead are physiognomically good –; but of this the Deponent knoweth not. As to my shape, 'tis a good shape enough, if measured – but my gait is awkward, and the walk, and the *Whole man* indicates

indolence capable of energies. – I am, and ever have been, a great reader – and have read almost every thing – a library-cormorant .... I compose very little – and I absolutely hate composition. Such is my dislike, that even a sense of Duty is sometimes too weak to overpower it.

I cannot breathe through my nose – so my mouth, with sensual thick lips, is almost always open. In conversation I am impassioned, and oppose what I deem error with an eagerness, which is often mistaken for personal asperity – but I am ever so swallowed up in the *thing*, that I perfectly forget my *opponent*. Such am I.

Other people's descriptions confirm his. Dorothy Words-worth thought him 'very plain' when she first saw him but the impression was dispelled as soon as he began talking:

His eye is large and full, not dark but grey; such an eye as would receive from a heavy soul the dullest expression; but it speaks every emotion of his animated mind; it has more of the 'poet's eye in a fine frenzy rolling' than I ever witnessed. He has fine dark eye-brows and an overhanging forehead.

The impact of Coleridge in full verbal flow is widely docu-mented. His oldest friend, Charles Lamb, recalled him as a senior boy at school, holding a group of fellow-pupils spellbound as he discoursed on some Classical theme in the cloisters. The young William Hazlitt heard him preach in Shrewsbury and was enthralled: 'I could not have been more delighted if I had heard the music of the spheres. Poetry and Philosophy had met together'. Thomas De Quincey, meeting him for the first time, found himself 'swept at once ... into a continuous strain of eloquent dissertation, certainly the most novel, the most finely illustrated, and traversing the most spacious fields of thought, by transitions the most just and logical, that it was possible to conceive'. Everyone remarked that dialogue with Coleridge had a strong tendency to become monologue, but no one – in the early years, at least – complained of that. He was one of the great talkers.

He was, in fact, one of those who talk their books away, who would rather hold forth in congenial company than sit alone at a desk in front of a blank sheet of paper. Writing is a lonely and demanding activity. You have to think all the time, and sometimes very hard. Anthony Burgess defined the writing process as 'an agony, mitigated by alcohol'. Its rewards are often small and there is no immediate audience to react, stimulate and encourage. Coleridge, by his own admission, hated composition. How much easier and pleasanter to sit comfortably among admiring friends and disciples, with the fire burning cheerfully and a bottle within reach, giving free rein to the flow of his natural eloquence. He once wrote to the political philosopher, William Godwin, apologising for getting drunk the night before and talking more wildly than usual:

> ... because tipsiness has, and has always, one unpleasant effect – that of making me talk *very* extravagently, and as when sober I talk extravagently enough for any *common* Tipsiness, it becomes a matter of nicety in discrimination to know when I am or am not affected.

There is something about writing about Coleridge that seems to lead to an excess of adjectives. The novelist Henry James, having read an early biography of Coleridge, wrote in his *Notebooks* of his 'rare, anomalous, magnificent, interesting, curious, tremendously suggestive character, vices and all'. Wordsworth said his friend was 'the most *wonderful* man that he had ever known', underlining the adjective – a man of wonders. De Quincey saluted 'the largest and most spacious intellect, the subtlest and most comprehensive, in my judgement, that has yet existed among men'.

It was the intellect that first impressed people – the breadth of his interests and references, the extent of his reading (in Greek, Latin and German as well as English), the richness and vitality of his imagery, his ability to draw fine distinctions in meaning, to see patterns and links in the unlikeliest of places.

But there was more to him than intellect alone. The phrase Coleridge coined to characterise Shakespeare, 'myriad-minded', describes him too. At his best, like Shakespeare, he was operating in those rarefied regions where mind and heart, thought and feeling, coalesce. For a brief period he could do it, almost intuitively, and though he then lost the ability, he never lost his conviction that it was at these intense moments that the poet approached closest to creative truth. In a letter written in March 1801 he said:

> My opinion is this – that deep Thinking is attainable only by a man of deep Feeling, and that all Truth is a species of Revelation. The more I understand of Sir Isaac Newton's works, the more boldly I dare utter to my own mind and therefore to *you*, that I believe the Souls of 500 Sir Isaac Newtons would go to the making up of a Shakespeare or a Milton.

Coleridge was not afraid to plumb the furthest depths of his own subconscious. And it is this unflinching perception that invests poems like 'Kubla Khan' and 'The Ancient Mariner' with such telling force. He was fascinated by his own dreams and nightmares, the powerful tides and currents that moved below the level of his conscious waking thoughts. And he had a highly developed sense of awe, of the numinous. He once remarked that man was the only animal that seemed to be struck with wonder. In the late summer of 1803, walking alone in the Scottish Highlands, he wrote in his *Notebook*:

> There have been times when looking up beneath the sheltring Trees, I could Invest every leaf with Awe.

Although Coleridge was a convinced Christian, he was also an inquiring one. His keen religious sense led him, in the middle years of his life when he was living in Keswick, to a kind of Pantheism. As much as Wordsworth, he felt himself at one with the natural world around him, part of a vast unity. Throughout his adult life he was searching for the key to what his instinct told him was the essential 'One-ness' of creation. In 1797 he wrote:

... the universe itself – what but an immense heap of *little* things? ... My mind feels as if it ached to behold something *great* – something *one* and *indivisible* – and it is only in the faith of this that rocks and waterfalls, mountains or caverns give me the sense of sublimity or majesty!

Four years later a single entry in the *Notebook* read: 'The great federal Republic of the Universe'.

Charles Lamb called Coleridge 'an archangel, a little damaged'. It was a characteristically charitable judgement. Coleridge was, in fact, very damaged indeed, in temperament: irresolute and irresponsible; incapable, for the most part, of adult self-discipline; dominating and demanding; full of high-sounding sentiments which his actions immediately belied; constantly outlining grandiose work plans that were doomed to come to nothing. He could not keep appointments. If he did keep them, he might be hours late. For all his widely recognised qualities as poet and preacher, lecturer and journalist, he could not make enough money to meet the basic needs of his family. Although everyone found Coleridge amazing and fascinating at first, those who lived in close daily contact with him soon found that he was always difficult, sometimes impossible. His great break with Wordsworth came in 1810 when he heard that his old friend had described him as hopeless, 'a rotten drunkard' who ran up debts at the alehouses, an 'absolute nuisance' about the home. Coleridge was deeply hurt when he heard this, all the more, one suspects, because he knew how much truth there was in the charges.

Various explanations have been proffered for these shortcomings – his mother's coldness, some trauma in infancy, his early exile from home and family, his later addiction to alcohol and opium. None of them seems entirely convincing on its own.

The chief problem in dealing with the early years of Coleridge's life is that he is the source of almost all the information available and, though he was capable of critical self-analysis, he was also inclined to self-justification. At first he appears to have been happy enough, the youngest of ten children and considerably spoilt as a result. He was a particular favourite of his father, vicar and headmaster of the grammar school at Ottery St Mary near Exeter, a man of learning and gentle benevolence. It is not clear what went wrong between Coleridge and his mother. At first he was her 'darling' but at some stage, apparently, there was a withdrawal of affection. Thereafter relations between them were cool. It may be for this reason that Coleridge grew up with a greater than usual need for approval, admiration and love. 'To be beloved is all I need,' he cried in his poem 'The Pains of Sleep'. There was much searching for a mother substitute.

Even so, until his tenth year, Coleridge was surrounded by a large, cheerful and affectionate family, with plenty of books to read and meadows and streams all around to explore. This all came to an abrupt end with the death of his father. Coleridge was sent, as a 'charity boy', to Christ's Hospital School in the City of London. It must have felt like being ejected from the Garden of Eden. In an age of brutal schooling, Christ's Hospital was notorious for the awfulness of its catering, the rigour of its discipline and the severity of its punishments. The headmaster, James Bowyer, was a relentless beater of boys but was also a dedicated teacher of Classics and poetry. Coleridge loved reading. With his precocious fluency and retentive mind for languages, he was quickly singled out as a boy destined to go on to university.

At Cambridge he started well. He studied hard and won a poetry prize. In his second year, though, he fell into dissolute ways, drinking, consorting with prostitutes, and – the French Revolution had just taken place – talking sedition with radical dons and students. He got into debt and, in December 1793, ran away to London and enlisted in the 15th Light Dragoons. It is the first clear sign of the temperamental instability that was to bedevil much of his later life. To run away at all was weakness; to join the army was folly; the choice of the cavalry was ridiculous. Coleridge was always a poor horseman, 'a very indocile Equestrian' as he phrased it. He gave himself a ludicrous alias, telling the army his name was Silas Tomkyn Comberbache. The retention of his initials is significant. He always disliked his

Christian names, preferring to be known either as Coleridge or as S.T.C.

The whole silly episode was probably no more than a cry for help and the help came quickly. His elder brothers traced him, bought his discharge, paid off his debts and restored him to Jesus College, Cambridge.

He returned, full of promises of reform, but they were not kept. He did not complete his degree course. Instead, he hurled himself into revolutionary politics. On a visit to Oxford he met a like-minded Balliol man, Robert Southey, and together they formed the core of an idealistic group which planned to establish a Utopian community, an 'experiment of human Perfectability', in the United States of America. A dozen young men, each with a wife, would cultivate virgin land on the banks of the Susquehanna River, all sharing in the daily labour, the rewards of that labour and in the decision-making. Coleridge devised a name for it: Pantisocracy, government by all. He was a man of high enthusiasms – 'Life were so flat a thing without Enthusiasm', he wrote – and he embraced the idea more whole-heartedly than any of the others.

Now he had to find himself a wife and he went about it in a typically feckless fashion. Southey and another of the Pantisocrats were engaged to two sisters who had another unattached sister, Sara Fricker, a lively and good-looking young woman. Before long Coleridge was engaged to her. He may have been a little in love with her – or persuaded himself that he was – or perhaps he simply hoped that love would grow as they got to know each other. He later claimed that he had, in fact, been in love with someone else at the time; that he had allowed his Pantisocratic zeal to carry him away; and that, when he tried to detach himself, Southey had railroaded him into honouring his engagement.

Coleridge and Sara married in Bristol in October 1795. They were happy at first. He was busy, talking endlessly, lecturing occasionally, editing and writing a political periodical. His earnings were meagre but rich friends, impressed by his genius, were more than generous. A son was born in September 1796 and Coleridge named him Hartley, after a philosopher he greatly admired. They lived in a tiny cottage at Nether Stowey, 5 miles from the Bristol Channel. He had been writing poetry for several years but it had been rather derivative, conventional verse. Now, inspired by his domestic happiness and his love of nature, he began to sound an individual note in blank verse poems like 'To the Nightingale' and 'The Eolian Harp', full of deep feeling but expressed in a gentle, musing, conversational tone.

There was an estrangement from Southey when it became clear that he was losing interest in the Pantisocracy project. Then Coleridge was swept away by a more inspiring friendship. Though he was better known as a poet than Wordsworth at that time, he had read some of Wordsworth's early efforts and been impressed by their style and novelty. The two men first met in September 1795. In June 1797 Coleridge, hearing that Wordsworth and his sister had rented a house in Dorset, covered the 40-mile journey on foot in 36 hours, vaulted over the field-gate, and exploded into their lives. It was meant to be a flying visit but he stayed for a fortnight. Soon after, the Wordsworths moved house to be closer to Coleridge. Many writers have described the ecstatic, inspirational quality of the three-way friendship – 'three persons with one soul', in Coleridge's phrase. There were long visits to each other's homes. They read their works aloud, both poems and plays. They talked endlessly, sitting up through the night, tramping about the Quantock hills. Friends were summoned to join them and share their delight. Mrs Coleridge, struggling to cope in a tiny cottage with her first baby and uncertain funds for the housekeeping, felt increasingly excluded.

The two young men began planning a joint volume of poetry and this was published, anonymously, under the title *Lyrical Ballads,* in September 1798. At first it had virtually no impact, on either the public or the critics. Very few readers – though Charles Lamb and Thomas De Quincey were honourably among them – saw it as marking the arrival of a new kind of English poetry. It is true that Wordsworth would go on to write more skilfully and more powerfully in the years that followed, but the unmistakable Wordsworthian tone was already clearly audible in many of these early poems, one of which, 'Tintern Abbey', has become an acknowledged and widely anthologised masterpiece. As for Coleridge, his main contribution to the collection, 'The Rime of the Ancient Mariner', is the poem for which he is now chiefly remembered. He had also written 'Kubla Khan' by this time but, like much of his work, it was unfinished and he did not publish it until 1816.

Soon after the book came out, William and Dorothy and Coleridge went to Germany. Coleridge, a natural European, knew that German philosophers, creative writers and literary critics were in the vanguard of the emergent Romantic movement. He wanted to master their language and read their works at first hand. Fascinated, he stayed in Germany for ten months, not even returning to his wife when the news reached him that their second son, Berkeley – also named after an admired philosopher – had died.

It is not surprising that, when he did finally arrive home again, he found the atmosphere strained. He was restless. He was still failing to meet his bread-winning responsibilities. He was full of grand notions about using his knowlege of advanced German thought to produce seminal works in English, but did nothing to implement them. When he heard that Wordsworth was ill, he hurried north to see him.

He found his friend, perfectly well, at a farm in County Durham, the home of the Hutchinson family, old friends of the Wordsworths. He loved the place and the people.

In November 1799 Wordsworth took Coleridge across the Pennines to show him the Lake District. It was an important trip for both of them. In the course of it, Wordsworth spotted the cottage on the outskirts of Grasmere, now known across the world as Dove Cottage, which was to be his home for the next few years. They walked vigorously, often in driving rain, along the valleys and over the ridges, admiring the landscape and deploring what Wordsworth called 'the New Erections and objects about Windermere'. For Coleridge the journey had the force of revelation. He wrote to Dorothy:

> You can feel what I cannot cannot express for myself –
> how deeply I have been impressed by a world of

scenery absolutely new to me. At Rydal and Grasmere I received I think the deepest delight, yet Hawes Water thro' many a varying view kept my eyes dim with tears, and this evening, approaching Derwentwater in diversity of harmonious features, in the majesty of its beauties and in the Beauty of its majesty – O my God! and the Black Crags close under the snowy mountains.... It was to me a vision of a fair Country.

He had walked among the mountains before, in North Wales when still a student, more recently in the Hartz Mountains of Germany. But the unique character of the Lake District fells – magnificent but also humanly manageable, varied and ever-changing – impressed him far more than anything he had seen before. Entries in his *Notebook* show him immediately embarking on his long experiment with language, trying to capture the evanescent impressions of light and season, the moving clouds and waters:

> ... The sunny mist, the luminous gloom of Plato ...
> ... Waterfall rolled after long looking at like a segment of a Wheel – the rock gleaming thro' it – Amid the roar a noise as of innumerable grasshoppers or of spinning wheels ...
> ... Distance removing all sense of motion or sound painted the waterfalls on the distant crags ...
> ... the hoar-frost on the ground, the lake calm and would have been mirrorlike but that it had been *breathed* on by the mist – and that shapely white Cloud, the Day-moon, hung over the snowy mountain opposite to us.

When he left the Lake District Coleridge did not go home but once again crossed the country to spend more time with the Hutchinsons. It was now that he fell in love with Sara, a plain and rather dumpy little woman but quick and lively-minded, full of fun and spirit. After her death, many years later, Wordsworth said she had had the quality of 'entertainingness'. Certainly, she now won Coleridge's heart and held it in thrall for the next ten years. In the physical sense, very little happened between them. They were both only too keenly aware of his married state. One evening, as the Hutchinson family stood round in the firelight, talking and joking, they held hands in secret. In his *Notebook* Coleridge wrote of:

The long Entrancement of a True-love's Kiss.

That was as far as it went. But for years his longing for the other Sara obsessed and perturbed him.

Tearing himself away at last, Coleridge went to London to earn money as a journalist, writing for the daily paper, the *Morning Post*. When the need was pressing and he put his mind to it, Coleridge could work with ferocious intensity. This he now did, producing a stream of articles on foreign affairs and political issues. In his spare time he was translating a play by Schiller.

The Wordsworths' decision to rent the cottage in Grasmere raised the question of where the Coleridges should settle. It could not be London, although that was where he could be sure of earning a reasonable living. One of his strongest beliefs, a recurring theme in his poems, was that children should be brought up in the country, free to roam and experience the world of nature. Mrs Coleridge, who was again pregnant, wanted to stay near Bristol, close to her family and friends, the shops and streets that she knew. But once the Wordsworths had made their decision, there was little doubt what Coleridge's would be. At the end of June 1800 the Coleridges and their worldly possessions travelled north.

It was Wordsworth who found Greta Hall, a big house on a hilltop close to the centre of Keswick and only 13 miles from Dove Cottage. The house – a large, very solid building in the late-Georgian style, with two curving wings – was still being built. It belonged to William Jackson, a local man who had recently retired from running a successful transport business. Jackson was so impressed by Coleridge when they met that he wanted to let him have the place free of charge, but Coleridge could not have that and they finally agreed on an annual rent of £40.

Greta Hall is splendidly situated, high enough to command the view in all directions, with the River Greta bending gracefully round the foot of the hill. The house is still there, hardly changed in its external appearance. The Coleridge family, and later the Southeys, were to live in it for more than 40 years. It is now, as it has been for nearly 80 years, a boarding house for girls at Keswick School, and the rooms where the poets lived and wrote are decorated with posters of pop groups and other heroes of modern youth.

On the final stage of their journey the Coleridges had stayed at Dove Cottage, and Coleridge described in a letter the evening picnic they had enjoyed on the lake:

> We drank tea the night before I left Grasmere on the Island in that lovely lake, our kettle swung over the fire hanging from the branch of a Fir Tree, and I lay and saw the woods, and mountains, and lake all trembling, and as it were *idealized* thro' the subtle smoke which rose up from the clear red embers of the fir-apples which we had collected. Afterwards, we made a glorious Bonfire on the Margin, by some alder bushes, whose twigs heaved and sobbed in the up-rushing column of smoke – and the Image of the Bonfire, and of us that danced round it – ruddy laughing faces in the twilight – the Image of this in a Lake smooth as that sea, to whose waves the Son of God had said, Peace!

He was in a state of euphoria, despite the fact that he had a heavy cold and a touch of rheumatic fever when they moved into Greta Hall. All his life Coleridge had ignored rain and dried out afterwards by steaming himself in front of the fire, still in his soggy clothes. As a result, the pains of rheumatism were the most persistent of his many ailments. Characteristically though, he never modified the habit, and never seems to have paused to wonder whether it was sensible for a man in his state of health to choose to live in the wettest corner of England.

As soon as he arrived in Keswick he poured out a stream of excited letters, urging his friends to come and see for themselves. To the scientist Humphry Davy, he wrote:

> ... 'Sdeath, my dear fellow! from the Window before me there is a great Camp of Mountains – Giants seem to have pitched their Tents there – each Mountain is a Giant's Tent – and how the light streams from them – and the Shadows that travel upon them!

And in another letter, he said:

> Right before me is a great *Camp* of single mountains – each in shape resembles a Giant's Tent! – and to the left ... is the lake of Keswick, with its Islands and white sails, and glossy Lights of Evening – crowned with green meadows, but the three remaining sides are encircled by the most fantastic mountains, that ever Earthquakes made in sport; as fantastic, as if Nature had *laughed* herself into the convulsion, in which they were made.

He loved the image of the Newlands mountains as a giants' encampment and it recurs again and again in his letters. Other images reappear as well: his son Hartley as 'a spirit that dances on an aspen leaf'; himself as 'Gentleman-poet and Philosopher in a mist'.

In the two years between Coleridge's arrival in Keswick and the start of his 'circumcursion' a lot happened to him and most of it was bad. He suffered much ill-health and it was in this period that he is said to have become addicted to opium, which he usually took in the liquid form of Kendal Black Drop, a more than commonly strong mixture of opium and alcohol. His family increased – another boy was born, called Derwent after Borrowdale's river – but the domestic discord increased as well. He was often away from home, sometimes for months on end – in London writing for the *Morning Post*, bathing in the North Sea to improve his health, staying with friends, especially the Hutchinsons. Relations with Mrs Coleridge deteriorated to the point of open conflict. This gave him digestive disorders; he took to drinking brandy in the evenings as well as laudanum; he found it hard to get to sleep and when he succeeded was visited by dreadful nightmares. And he could no longer write poetry. He had a prolonged struggle to complete the eerie narrative of 'Christabel' which Wordsworth had said would be included in the new edition of *Lyrical Ballads*. 'Every line has been produced by me with labor-pangs', Coleridge said. He was reduced to near despair when Wordsworth decided the poem would not be included after all. In one terrifying *Notebook* entry, dated 30th October 1800, he wrote:

> He knew not what to do – something, he felt, must be done – he rose, drew his writing-desk suddenly before him – sate down, took the pen – and found that he knew not what to do.

Unable to compose, he occupied his mind by reading philosophy and conducting scientific experiments suggested by Humphry Davy.

Even so, in the midst of all this, he continued to pour out letters that, although they gave full details of all his afflictions, were also sparkling with ideas and jokes and bright images and enthusiasms. And when he was well enough, he went fell-walking.

They were all formidable walkers. None of them, in the early years, could afford horses and carriages. The Wordsworths thought nothing of walking the 13 miles over Dunmail Raise and past Thirlmere to spend a few hours at Greta Hall before setting off back to Dove Cottage. Southey, when he came to live in Keswick, claimed he could maintain 3 miles an hour and read a book at the same time; if he closed the book, his speed went up to 4 miles an hour. But Coleridge could out-walk them all. He was their superior in vigour, stamina and, most important, in boldness.

Nowadays, when you find six-year-olds on the highest mountain tops and octogenarians striding along the ridges, it is hard to credit the trepidation, terror even, which steep rough ground inspired in the breasts of virtually everyone at that time. Even the rumbustious Captain Budworth had to bind up one eye as he descended the Langdale Pikes. Mrs Ann Radcliffe, queen of the 'Gothick horror' school of novel writing, hired a guide and horses to get her to the top of Skiddaw from the Keswick side and, approaching the summit, reported chasms, torrents and precipices that made her 'recoil from the view with involuntary horror'. It sounds like the novelist still at work, but that was the way almost everyone reacted to the fells until well into the nineteenth century. In a way such accounts are a tribute to the power of the human imagination: the things they saw were not there on the ground, but very much there in their minds. It is all too easy to deride them, but theirs was the prevailing spirit of the time. It called for great psychological strength to break through it.

Coleridge did so straight away. As soon as he was settled into Greta Hall he was off to explore the mountains all around, undeterred by bad weather or poor visibility: 'The wind from Skiddaw and Borrowdale was often as loud as wind need be – and many a walk in the clouds on the mountains did I take.' Sometimes when he went to visit the Wordsworths he would turn off the road to make his way along the ridge to the summit of Helvellyn, where he would admire the sunset and then stumble down to Grasmere in darkness. He preferred to walk alone: '. . . for I must be alone, if either my Imagination or Heart are to be excited or enriched'.

In the summer of 1801 he wrote:

> Scenes in Easedale, rocks and woods, and trees starting up around Rocks and out of Rocks – where under the Boughs and through the Boughs you have the glimmering Lake, and Church Tower . . . To wander and wander for ever and ever . . .

He filled his *Notebooks* with everything he saw and felt: the names of mountains and wild flowers; snippets of local lore and history; descriptions of the great panoramic views, swirling clouds and changing lights, alongside pen-portraits of ferns and mosses and other tiny details. And all the time he was analysing the landscape and his responses to it, searching for parallels and connections and lessons, asking questions. In a letter he compared the view of the Newlands fells from his study window to Snowdon in North Wales:

> ... I know of no mountain in the *north* altogether equal to Snowdon, but then we have an *encampment* of huge Mountains, in no harmony perhaps to the eye of a mere painter, but always interesting, various and, as it were, nutritive.

Other *Notebook* jottings include:

> ... slanting pillars of misty light moved along under the Sun hid by clouds ...
> ... Leaves of Trees upturned by the stirring wind in twilight – an image for paleness from affright ...
> ... Nature's pictures all in motion = shadows ...
> ... N.B. What is it that makes the silent *bright* of the Morning vale so different from that other silence and bright gleams of late evening? Is it in the mind or is there any physical cause?

In the first volume of his biography of Coleridge, Richard Holmes says:

> These prose notations were a new form of Romantic nature-writing, as powerful in their way as his poetry; rapid, spontaneous, miraculously responsive to the changing panorama of hills he moves through, and containing a sort of telegraphic score of his emotional reactions.

The primary sources for Coleridge's big fell-walk lie in his letters and his *Notebook* entries, and I think it was here that he was now doing his best writing. He himself believed that what he called 'the shaping Spirit of Imagination' – which had enabled him to write the great conversational poems like 'Frost at Midnight' and 'This Lime Tree Bower my Prison', and evoke the dream-like worlds of 'Kubla Khan' and 'The Ancient Mariner' – had deserted him. In March 1801 he wrote to a friend:

> The Poet is dead in me – my imagination (or rather the somewhat that had been imaginative) lies, like

Cold Snuff on the circular Rim of a Brass Candle-
stick, without even a stink of Tallow to remind you
that it was once cloathed and mitred with Flame.

This very passage, like many others, makes it abundantly
clear that he could still summon up brilliant, apt and unexpected
images, a vital and vitalising element in poetry. Yet for some
reason, when he tried to apply this power to the writing of
poetry, he ran out of confidence, could not complete the work.
In despair, he turned to the more intellectual, arid fields of
philosophy and science, and later to literary criticism and
theology, producing works that seem, to me at least, impene-
trably dense and difficult.

In the *Notebooks,* though, we have Coleridge talking to
himself, thinking directly on to the paper. In his letters we hear
him talking to his friends. Reading both, we approach as close
as we can ever hope to get to his thought processes as they
happened. It is almost like listening to the great talker in full
conversational flow.

CHAPTER TWO

The Walk Begins

On Sunday Augt. 1st – ½ after 12 I had a Shirt, cravat, 2 pair of Stockings, a little paper and half a dozen Pens, a German Book [Voss's Poems] and a little Tea and Sugar, with my Night cap, packed up in my natty green oil-skin, neatly squared, and put into my *net* Knapsack and the Knap-sack on my back and the Besom stick in my hand, which for want of a better, and in spite of Mrs. C. and Mary, who both raised their voices against it, especially as I left the Besom scattered on the Kitchen Floor, off I sallied – over the Bridge, thro' the Hop-Field, thro' the Prospect Bridge at Portinscale, so on by the tall Birch that grows out of the center of the huge Oak, along into Newlands – ...

It was with this headlong sentence that Coleridge began the first of his two long letters to Sara Hutchinson, describing his walk. The original letters are lost, but, luckily, Sara thought them interesting enough to be transcribed into a journal and that has survived. She omitted the more personal passages – he usually opened with 'My dearest Sara' and ended with blessings and protestations of love – but she faithfully copied out the details of his journey and even tried to reproduce his occasional, rather clumsy drawings.

It seems a little odd that he took no change of shirt with him, but the most notable absence from his list is that of any mention of laudanum. According to the biographies he was already seriously addicted to opium by this stage. It is hard to believe that such a man could have contemplated many days of deprivation. Coleridge was not, by nature, a self-denying man. On the contrary, his inclination was to self-indulgence. Perhaps he did put a bottle of Kendal Black Drop in his knapsack, and for some reason omitted it from his list. The reason would not be shame; his letters are full of references to laudanum. And he certainly knew that if his craving grew too strong on the journey, he could always buy some at the next chemist's shop he passed. It was available, without prescription, as aspirins are today. But the fact remains that in all he wrote about the walk there is not a word about drinking laudanum, or brandy either. It is tempting to conclude that, probably for the last time in his life, he found he could get along with no more stimulation than that afforded by vigorous exercise, fresh air and the excitements of the journey.

That first sentence of his letter gives the impression that he set off on a sudden impulse. It was not so. It may have been a last-minute decision to go exactly when he did, but his *Notebook* makes it clear that he had been planning a long walk around the western side of the Lake District for some time.

Over several pages, before the start of the walk, we find him trying to fix the topography of the region in his mind, the pattern of its rivers, distances involved, points of interest en route:

> ... Enquire in Eskdale for Buck Crag, Doe Crag and Earn Crag.
> ... When in Miterdale, try by all means to command a view of Ravenglass.
> ... Enquire at Muncaster for the Children's Ditty on New Year's Eve, craving the Bounty they were wont to have in good King Edward's Days

Notes like this make it clear that Coleridge had been studying the monumental but not always reliable *History and Antiquities of Cumberland*, written in two volumes by William Hutchinson and published in 1794. Hutchinson's work included a map of Cumberland, and Coleridge made a ham-fisted attempt to copy it into his *Notebook*. It was all he had to guide him.

It is obvious from his preparatory notes that he intended to spend three days or so at St Bees, inspecting a collection of old books he had heard about. He also planned to return home by way of Sty Head Pass and Borrowdale, the path he had followed with Wordsworth in 1799. In these two respects he was to diverge from his plans. The rest of his journey, remarkably for Coleridge, was very much as he intended.

His aim on the first day was to cross over Newlands Pass and drop down to the valley of Buttermere, then – striking due west – to cross Floutern Pass and descend to the village of Ennerdale Bridge. It is more than 18 miles and involves well over 2,000 feet of ascent and descent. It says much for Coleridge's confidence as a walker that he did not set off until after midday. But he knew the route – he had walked it before – and he knew where he would sleep that night. His Keswick landlord, William Jackson, had given him a note of introduction to John Ponsonby, an elderly farmer who lived at Long Moor, a mile or so beyond Ennerdale Bridge.

I knew the route too, but I had no idea where I would sleep that night. The only thing I could be sure of was that Ennerdale Bridge would be crowded with visitors on a Sunday night in mid-August because it is the first halting-place on the coast-to-coast walk from St Bees to Robin Hood's Bay on the North Sea coast. The walk was devised by the late A. Wainwright and has grown in popularity every year since he published his guidebook to it in 1973.

Wainwright is an inescapable figure in the modern Lake District, not by sight – he was rarely spotted even in the days when he haunted the fells with his notebook and camera – but by name and reputation. He became famous between the mid-1950s and the mid-'60s, when the seven pocket-sized volumes of his *Pictorial Guides to the Lakeland Fells* were being published. More than a million copies have been sold. Every second person that you come across in the fells seems to be 'walking with Wainwright', stopping frequently to consult the appropriate page of the appropriate volume to make sure he is still on the correct Wainwright-recommended path and missing none of the things he should be noticing.

There are some – mostly people who started fell-walking in the pre-Wainwright era – who denounce the man and all his works. He has made their sport, they say, too safe and easy and too readily available to all comers. The thrills and satisfactions of personal exploration have been lost. There is no longer any call for skills in map-reading and compass work. It has become increasingly difficult, in the main holiday periods, to find the things that attracted Wordsworth and Coleridge and countless successors to the mountains – communion with nature, solitude and silence, time to walk and observe and think without constant human interruption. The fells, they claim, are grossly over-crowded and seriously eroded, and the man responsible is Wain-wright.

The argument is elitist and largely specious. It is undeniable that the popular routes are sometimes overcrowded and that many paths have been eroded. But this was happening long before Wainwright's books began to come out, and would have gone on happening, at an accelerating rate, had he never written a word. The prime causes are social and economic – longer holidays, earlier retirement, faster roads, many more motor cars. Had Wainwright never been born, new and more detailed fell-walking guidebooks to the Lake District would undoubtedly have been published. The chances are that they would not have been so informative and sensible and entertaining as his books are, nor so visually unusual and attractive, nor so alive with crusty character.

When he completed his work in Lakeland, Wainwright turned his attention to longer walks elsewhere in northern England and produced a pictorial guidebook to the Pennine Way. He worked out the coast-to-coast route and did a book about that. It was this that threatened to make life difficult for me on the first night of my walk. Long before I set off I felt sure that one of the chief differences between Coleridge's journey and mine would be the problem of finding accommodation. I was proved right. It was one area in which Coleridge had the advantage over me.

There were others. He was two and a half months short of his thirtieth birthday; I was two months beyond my sixty-third. He was widely regarded as an original genius; and no one, to my knowledge, has ever said such a thing about me. I grew up in Bolton, Lancashire; served briefly and without distinction, in the infantry; read Modern History, under A. J. P. Taylor, at

Oxford after the Second World War; then worked for many years as a journalist – on a provincial evening newspaper, then for the Nigerian Broadcasting Corporation, then with ITN in London. I grew fond of mountains and mountaineering and wrote a few books on the subject. In 1975 I resigned from ITN because I wanted to live in the Lake District. I have done so ever since, earning a precarious living as a writer of books and articles and radio programmes, an occasional lecturer, a mountain guide in the holiday season.

If Coleridge had youth on his side, the advantage lay with me in all other respects. He was an ailing man much of the time and taking too much opium; I was fit from a summer of mountain walking and swimming and tennis, and, though not averse to alcohol, not hopelessly dependent on it either. His domestic situation was fundamentally unhappy, although things were slightly better at this time and his wife was pregnant once more; my home life was, by comparison, serene. He was finding it impossible to write, whereas I had just completed a history of Lake District rock-climbing, had a book to do about a battle in the American Civil War, and was now starting research for yet another book.

In terms of equipment, it was no contest. His sole aids to route-finding were the map he had roughly copied into his *Notebook* and his innate sense of direction. I carried a compass and all the appropriate 1:25,000 Ordnance Survey maps. I had a whistle to summon help, and the reassuring knowledge that, if I got into difficulties, there would almost certainly be other people along shortly. If the accident were serious, the volunteers of the Mountain Rescue Service would be on the spot before long. Coleridge could be equally sure that, if he had a disabling accident in the hills, the chances of his being discovered in time were very remote.

He had a knapsack slung across one shoulder, while my gear was all packed into a commodious and comfortable rucksack, with a rolled-up lightweight mattress perched on top in case I failed to find a bed. My Gore-Tex anorak was warm and windproof and as waterproof as modern textile technology can get, with plenty of pockets. I wore climbing breeches, warm and flexible, and two pairs of thick woollen stockings. My boots were light and comfortable and waterproof, giving a firm grip on all types of terrain.

Coleridge tells us little about his clothing, beyond the items mentioned at the start of his letter. It is safe to assume, however, that he wore stout country boots of strong and supple leather, with steel nails screwed into the soles and heels. Later entries in his *Notebooks* show him to have been something of a theorist about footwear, working out in detail the types of leather to be used, the best preparations for it, the kind of nails required and how they should be patterned. Coleridge had done enough mountain walking to know that boots are the first priority. He probably had a good, comfortable pair, well broken in. He seems to have suffered no discomfort during his 'circumcursion', and on the last day he walked nearly as far as he had on the first.

The Lake District is famous for its weather. Its best days are incomparable; its bad ones can be dreadful; and it can switch, very quickly, from one extreme to the other.

Records show that the general weather pattern has hardly changed in two centuries. One of Coleridge's Keswick contemporaries was an eccentric, industrious and prickly-tempered little man called Peter Crosthwaite, the first in the area to see and seize the opportunities arising from the tourist industry. He opened the town's first museum; he drew very good maps of the lakes, indicating the best viewpoints (then called 'stations'), and sold them to the visitors; he laid out a zig-zag path up Latrigg to make the ascent easy; for ten years running he was commander of the fleet that invaded the northernmost island on Derwentwater and staged a mock sea-battle, with much firing of cannon and shouting of oaths, on Regatta Day. He also kept careful records of the weather. In 1793 he recorded just under 59 inches of rain; an average temperature of just under 48 degrees Fahrenheit; a prevailing wind from the south-west; and, taking sightings three times a day, established that the summit of Skiddaw was hidden by cloud more than half the time. In all respects, things are much the same now in an average year.

But 1989 was far from being an average year. The previous

winter had been very mild and wet. From mid-April onwards, however, the District had almost unremitting sunshine and scarcely a drop of rain. By the beginning of August the lakes were shrunken but warm enough for leisurely bathing; there was grass growing in the riverbeds; the most notorious stretches of marshland and peat bog could be crossed, in trainers, with no danger of wet feet. The long dry spell came to an end, resoundingly, on the day I set off.

I woke before 8 a.m. and saw the branches of the oak trees across the road swaying violently, lashed by wind and rain. The sky was grey-black. The slopes of Skiddaw were invisible, enveloped in swirling vapour. The radio weather forecast had nothing better to promise than a day-long deterioration. Experience as a mountain guide had taught me not to take these predictions too much to heart. It had often seemed to me that the forecasters, ever since their failure to give a sufficiently weighty warning of the hurricane that uprooted millions of trees in southern and central England in 1987, had taken refuge in always erring on the pessimistic side. Time and again I had found that, however bad the weather when you set off and however gloomy the prognostications, if you march boldly forth you will be rewarded, nine times out of ten, with a tolerable, even an enjoyable day, and will not end up soaked to the skin. There is always the tenth time, however. And Sunday, 13th August 1989, was one of them.

Soon after 10 a.m. I shouldered the rucksack and made my way to Greta Hall. It was raining, but not too heavily. Farewells were said, and I set off at 10.15 down the hill and between the buildings of Keswick School, turned right on the main road, crossed the stone bridge over the River Greta, then swung left to leave the road and gain the flat meadows that lead to the village of Portinscale. This was the route Coleridge had taken. There were very few people about.

I heard the bells of Crosthwaite Church calling the faithful to Sunday morning service. Through the rain, darkly, I could just discern the outline of the square tower. The church was there when Coleridge passed by – according to legend there has been a place of Christian worship on the spot since St Kentigern (also known as Mungo) arrived from Scotland and planted the cross in 553 AD. But Coleridge makes no mention of it. Although he was a deeply Christian man, he was no regular churchgoer. And surprisingly, for a man of such wide-ranging curiosity, he showed no interest in church architecture. The Lake District is rich in intriguing old churches and he passed several on his walk but ignored them all.

The hopfield he speaks of is no longer there. Neither is the Prospect Bridge across the River Derwent. In those days, and for a further century and more, the bridge was on the main road linking Keswick with Cockermouth and the west coast. It was also a popular spot for painters and 'picturesque' visitors, an ancient stone bridge with two hump-backed arches. There were moves to have it replaced with something more modern in the years before the First World War, but they were strenuously and successfully opposed by the Vicar of Crosthwaite, the campaigning Canon Hardwicke Drummond Rawnsley, one of the heroes of the story of Lake District conservation. Someone celebrated his success with an appropriate adaptation of Macaulay's lines about Horatius:

> With weeping and with laughter
> Still is the story told
> How Hardie Rawnsley kept the bridge
> In the brave days of old.

The Canon had the old bridge strengthened and it stood for another 40 years, until its main buttress was swept away in the autumn floods of 1954. In its place there now stands an incongruous metal suspension bridge, for pedestrians only, which bounces pleasantly under your feet if you bang them down hard.

Another thing that Coleridge mentions – 'the tall Birch that grows out of the center of the huge Oak' – is not there now. Indeed, it may not have been a birch at all. Captain Budworth spotted the phenomenon ten years before, and wrote:

> Before we reached the brook, we saw a treble-trunked
> oak: the centre trunk was hollow, and a mountain ash

grew out of it; about two yards down it we broke a hole with our sticks, and the ash was strong and healthy.

The village of Portinscale, a mile west of Keswick, is at least 1,000 years old. Etymologists, who seem very sure of themselves, say the name derives from the old Norse language and means 'the hut of the prostitute'. For a place of such antiquity, it has an oddly foreign feel to it. You walk between a couple of big hotels, built in the grand Victorian manner, and past the village shop; catch a glimpse of terraced cottages that were there when Coleridge walked by; then proceed along a leafy road lined with mid-twentieth-century detached bungalows, each with its carefully tended front garden and a blaze of herbaceous borders and flowering shrubs. Further on there is a yacht club on the lakeshore and then a marine centre. It does not feel like the Lake District, more like one of the flourishing Home County suburbs that John Betjeman celebrated in his poems.

On the outskirts of the village there is a big house, Derwent Bank, which belongs to the Holiday Fellowship and is visited each year by thousands of enthusiastic fell-walkers. I passed a long crocodile of them, heading towards Keswick, walkers of all ages in sturdy boots and shorts and brightly coloured waterproofs, exuding the sort of loud jocularity that seems to be inescapable whenever keen ramblers and atrocious weather coincide. I wondered what Coleridge would have made of this modern version of his solitary, reflective pastime.

In 1802 the route over Newlands Pass was no more than a bridle path. Those who travelled by carriage, as most tourists did, had to go the longer way to Buttermere, over Whinlatter Pass to the north. Both are motor roads now but very different. The Whinlatter way takes you through the massed and serried ranks of Forestry Commission conifers. That over Newlands begins with leafy lanes; opens out into a lovely green valley, with varied mountain scenery all round; then gains height to emerge on to a bleak heathland that leads to the summit of the pass. There were no conifer forests in Whinlatter 200 years ago, but even then the author of the first guide to the Lake District, a Jesuit priest called Thomas West, preferred the quicker route: '... whoever takes a ride up Newlands Vale will be agreeably surprized with some of the finest solemn pastoral scenes they have yet beheld'. And William Gilpin, the theorist of 'the picturesque', remarked upon the smoothness of the mountain slopes in this region:

> The mountain valleys we had hitherto seen were rocky, wild and desolate; but here the idea of terror was excluded. The valley of Newlands was even adorned with the beauties of luxuriant nature. We travelled through groves which were sometimes open and sometimes close, with a sparkling stream, the common attendant of these valleys, accompanying us through the whole scene.

The scene hereabouts is still little changed, apart from the metalled road and the traffic on it. This is how Coleridge described it in his letter to Sara Hutchinson:

> ... Newlands is indeed a lovely Place – the houses, each in it's little Shelter of Ashes and Sycamores, just under the Road so that in some places you might leap down on the Roof, seemingly at least – the exceeding greenness and pastoral beauty of the Vale itself, with the savage wildness of the Mountains, their Coves, and long arm-shaped and elbow-shaped Ridges – yet this wildness softened down into a congruity with the Vale by the semicircular Lines of the Crags, and of the bason-like Concavities.

The name Newlands originated, they say, in medieval times when the extensive swamps of the valley floor were drained and cleared of boulders to create good 'new land'. In the sixteenth and seventeenth centuries this area stood at the heart of the great mining boom, and the scars are still very visible on the fellsides – spoil heaps of rubble where nothing will grow, dark tunnels driving into the hillsides, derelict buildings. Lower down, it is pure pasture land, a smiling valley and – even by the demanding standards of the Lake District – uncommonly rich in literary associations.

In its lower reaches, along the lakeside between Portinscale and the slopes of the mountain called Cat Bells, the young Beatrix Potter enjoyed long summer holidays. The story of her life is perhaps more remarkable and more moving than any of the tales she wrote for children, and it had a reassuringly happy ending. Her parents were well-off and leisured, intensely conventional and domineering. Beatrix spent her childhood and adolescence and early womanhood as their virtual prisoner, comfortable and looked after but allowed no freedom. She did not go to school. She had no friends of her own age. Most of the time was spent quietly and studiously, in her upstairs room in Kensington.

Half a century before, John Ruskin had endured a similar upbringing and the effects on both of them were similar. They were each forced into their own tiny worlds and developed great powers of concentration; they studied and drew the minutiae around them, the patterns in the carpet, in rocks and stones, ferns and lichens, mice and snails and birds' feathers. For Beatrix the summer holidays in Scotland and the Lake District meant an unaccustomed freedom to explore, observing everything. Several of her early tales are set in the landscape of this part of the northern Lake District. And it was a holiday friend of the family, the Reverend H. D. Rawnsley (later, Canon Rawnsley, and the Vicar of Crosthwaite), who first encouraged her to publish her stories.

The money she made from the sale of her books finally, in middle age, enabled her to break away from her parents. She bought a farm at Sawrey, near Hawkshead, in the southern Lake District, and became a countrywoman. She married a local solicitor, acquired more farms and devoted herself to the breeding and rearing of the traditional sheep of the District, the Herdwick. She had no interest in the tales she had written before the First World War (apart from the money they were still bringing in), and would not waste her time in literary discussion. In 1933 when Graham Greene published a deeply researched and very complimentary essay about her work, he was rewarded with an acidulous little note from Sawrey correcting a few minor errors, denying that a change in her work had been the result of a great emotional upset, and deprecating what she called 'the Freudian school of criticism'.

When she died in 1943 she left her Herdwick sheep and her farms – more than 4,000 acres of land – to the National Trust, a final thank you to her old mentor Canon Rawnsley who had been one of the founders of the National Trust.

I doubt whether Beatrix Potter ever looked at any of Hugh Walpole's novels, and I feel reasonably sure that if she had she would not have liked them. Coleridge, too, would almost certainly have disapproved. For Walpole's syntax is often sloppy, his use of words imprecise, the whole quality of mind mushy and sentimental. Yet his four-volume melodramatic saga of Lake District life, *The Herries Chronicle*, has been continuously in print for more than half a century. He had the storyteller's vital gifts: narrative pace and vigour; the ability to create characters and dramatic scenes; the feeling for period and a strong sense of atmosphere, especially where evil and torture and pain were involved. He was one of those rare writers who actually enjoyed writing. The words gushed from his pen as he sat in his study on the lower slopes of Cat Bells, looking across the treetops and the 'shining levels' of Derwentwater to the mountains beyond. He had no time for revision – like his readers he was too eager to know what was going to happen next in the story.

He discovered the house, Brackenburn, in 1923, bought it on the spot and, after his fashion, loved the place; he called it his 'little paradise'. He explored the fell country around, read deep into its history and described it as 'an enchanted place'. Though he was often away – he could never long resist the lure of metropolitan life, the opera houses of Europe, the literary gossip of London – when he was at Brackenburn he threw himself, with characteristic gusto and generosity, into local life. He died in June 1941, having exhausted himself by making a long march through the streets of Keswick and a speech in the park at the opening of War Weapons' Week. It is one of the unsolved mysteries of our time that no television company has yet transformed the Herries story into a swashbuckling costume serial.

The important Coleridge connection in the Newlands region, however, is the writer Molly Lefebure who lives in a remote farmhouse high up in the valley. When I passed that way in the summer of 1989 she was said to be researching the life of Hartley Coleridge, whose adulthood was blighted by alcohol in something of the same way in which his father's had been blighted by opium. Three years earlier she had published a biography of Mrs Coleridge, persuasively defending her from the many charges and calumnies that her husband heaped upon her. Before that, in 1974, Mrs Lefebure had brought out *Samuel Taylor Coleridge: a Bondage of Opium*, using her professional knowledge of the modern problems of drug addiction to create a vivid reinterpretation of his life.

It is a fascinating and thoroughly researched book, though, in my opinion, it puts too much emphasis on the influence of his opium addiction. Beyond doubt, it was a very influential and damaging element in his life. But Coleridge displayed a basic temperamental instability, a capacity for irresponsibility and wild impulsiveness, long before he can be said to have become an addict. His addiction, I believe, was a symptom rather than the cause of his flawed character.

For all this, Mrs Lefebure's book is strongly argued and stimulating. And I have no quarrel at all with an earlier judgement of hers, in an essay called 'The First of the Fellwalkers' which concluded with these words:

> Although his career as a fellwalker was of comparatively short duration, his exploits on the hills were wholly remarkable, his attitude to high places revolutionary and his notebooks covering the period remain unrivalled as prose writing about the Lake District.

He should be honoured, she claims, as 'the patron saint of fellwalkers'.

The waterfall at the top of Newlands Pass, Moss Force, was disappointing when Coleridge went by. 'The cataract', he said, 'had but little water in it.' Consequently, he found it 'of no particular Interest'. He liked his cataracts to be in tumultuous spate. He would have admired it as it was when I passed. It was visible from a mile down the valley, a white gash cascading down the northern slope of Buttermere Moss. Getting closer, I could make out the two black boulders that split the tumbling waters, and great clouds of spray being hurled across the crag face by the fiercer gusts.

The wind was driving the rain straight into my face. It felt as though a measurable proportion of the Atlantic Ocean was being directed, maliciously, at me alone. The stronger gusts would stop me in my tracks. A few cars crept by, all with their lights on full beam, and the passengers craned their necks to gaze at me, more in amazement, it seemed, than sympathy. None of them offered a lift.

I was two hours into the walk by this time and very wet. Initially there had been some shelter from roadside trees and one or two moments when it looked as if the storm might be subsiding. I remembered Wordsworth's fine sentence in his *Guide through the District of the Lakes*: 'The rain here comes down heartily, and is frequently succeeded by clear, bright weather, when every brook is vocal and every torrent sonorous.' It was coming down heartily all right, but there was now no sign of the promised sequel. Although my anorak protected my body, I had lost the hood and was wearing an old duvet hat that simply soaked up the water. I had to take it off and wring it out – a gallon or so at a time – every 15 minutes. The rucksack was taking in water, too, and getting noticeably heavier. I had no waterproof over-trousers so the rain poured off my anorak, soaked into my breeches and down through my stockings to settle in puddles around my feet. Suddenly, the fact that the boots were waterproof was a disadvantage.

As I hurried down to Buttermere two cyclists passed me going the other way, using the wind to help push them uphill. Apart from the crocodile of ramblers I had passed on the outskirts of Keswick, these were the only people I had seen on the 9-mile march who were not cowering in their cars.

The car parks in Buttermere were full and so was the long

extension bar at the back of the Fish Hotel. I hung up my anorak and duvet hat, got a pint of Guinness and a bowl of vegetable soup, and found myself a corner of a table.

Compared to the more developed valleys of the District, Buttermere has a remote and rural feel to it. When Coleridge was there the Fish was the only inn; there were a few farms and cottages and the tiny stone-built chapel, which he ignored. Thomas West had said:

> The life of the inhabitants is purely pastoral. A few
> hands are employed in the slate quarries; the women
> spin woollen yarn and drink tea.

In fact, as in most of the quieter valleys, the population was greater then than it is now. Farming was entirely a matter of human labour, with some help from dogs and horses. The quarries were busy and, in some parts, the mines were still being worked. Cottage industry went on and in many places there were water-driven mills, turning wood or weaving rough cloth.

One of the things that makes the Lake District especially intriguing is the fact that, although it is a small region which – at first sight – appears homogeneous, each of the main valleys has its own quite distinctive character. Borrowdale is broad and variegated and richly wooded, with many dwellings in view and a backcloth of black crags and high mountains, some rounded, some jagged. It feels dramatic and yet friendly. Buttermere, by contrast, is altogether grander and more imposing in its effects. There are few trees and fewer buildings. The hills are massy, smooth-sloped and all-enclosing. The atmosphere is barer and bleaker.

Coleridge brought his power of original imagery to bear when he sought to give Sara Hutchinson some idea of the Buttermere valley:

> Conceive an enormous round Bason mountain-high
> of solid Stone cracked in half and one half gone,
> exactly in the remaining half of this enormous Bason
> does Buttermere lie in this beautiful and stern Em-
> bracement of Rock.

In his *Guide to the Lakes* Thomas West, although a Jesuit priest in a fiercely Protestant land, contrasted Buttermere with the high valleys of the European Alps very much to the former's advantage:

> Here, if the roads in some places be narrow and difficult, they are at least safe. No villainous banditti haunt the mountains; innocent people live in the dells. Every cottager is narrative of all he knows; and mountain virtue and pastoral hospitality are found at every farm. This constitutes a pleasing difference betwixt travelling here and on the continent, where every innholder is an extortioner, and every voiturin an imposing rogue.

By a remarkable coincidence, it so happens that there was 'an imposing rogue' in Buttermere on the day when Coleridge passed through. They had not met and they did not meet now, but, in the year that followed, Coleridge – in his role as journalist – was to play a leading part in the man's detection and downfall.

His real name was John Hatfield but he had been introducing himself as Alexander Augustus Hope, an army colonel, MP for Linlithgowshire and younger brother of the Earl of Hopetoun. He was handsome, had a ready wit, and travelled in an impressive carriage. His manner was aristocratic but courteous. It is not surprising that his appearance in Keswick in the summer of 1802 should have created a minor sensation. He charmed most of the women and many of the men, borrowed money freely and ran up big bills at the Queen's Head Hotel. In fact, he was looking for a wealthy and well-connected wife and the search did not take long. He was soon engaged to a young heiress.

He must have heard of Coleridge, who was well-known in Keswick and respected as a poet and philosopher. But he kept well clear of him. Some have suggested that this was because Hatfield was a West Countryman and feared recognition. More likely, although confident that he could fool most of the people most of the time, he did not feel so sure that he could humbug a man of Coleridge's intelligence, perception and knowledge of the world.

At the end of July, Hatfield left Keswick for a few days' fishing for char, a Lake District delicacy, in the deep waters of Buttermere. He stayed at the Fish Inn – there was nowhere else – and so, inevitably, he met the landlord's daughter Mary Robinson.

Mary was 24 years old, unmarried, something of an innocent, and something of a celebrity too. It was Captain Joseph Budworth who had made her famous. He stayed at the Fish in the course of his *Fortnight's Ramble* in 1792, and described her enthusiastically:

> She brought in part of our dinner, and seemed to be about 15. Her hair was thick and long, of a dark brown, and, though unadorned with ringlets, did not seem to want them; her face was a fine oval, with full eyes and lips as red as vermilion; her cheeks had more of the lily than the rose .... When we first saw her at her distaff, after she had got the better of her first fears, she looked an angel; and I doubt not but she is the reigning lily of the valley.

Before long Mary was a considerable tourist attraction, widely known as 'The Beauty of Buttermere'. To a country girl, naturally modest in manner, who had never been away from home, it was all very embarrassing. It seems probable that Hatfield went to Buttermere not only to fish but to see Mary. What is certain is that the moment he saw her he fell so hopelessly in love that the accomplished conman forgot his fortune-hunting plans on the spot. He very quickly won her heart.

His wooing must have been proceeding exactly when Coleridge was there. If he saw either of the lovers, however, he made no note of it. To Sara Hutchinson he merely wrote:

> ... came out on Buttermere and drank Tea at the little Inn, and read the greater part of the Revelations.

This was the Book of Revelations in the New Testament. After resting and reading for an hour or so, he went on his way.

For Mary and Hatfield, events moved swiftly in the next

few weeks. Within two months they were married. Local interest was aroused by the speed of the affair, the handsome appearance of the principals, most of all by the social daring of their alliance. It was a very rare event in those days of strict class divisions for a simple country girl to win the hand of a man of (apparently) high social position. Convinced that it would be of more than regional interest, Coleridge wrote a piece about it for the *Morning Post*. It was entitled 'The Romantic Marriage' and opened with the words:

> On the 2nd instant a Gentleman, calling himself Alexander Augustus Hope, Member for Linlithgowshire and brother to the Earl of Hopetoun, was married at the church of Lorton near Keswick to a young woman celebrated by the tourists under the name of The Beauty of Buttermere ...

The careful wording suggests that Coleridge already had some doubts about the identity of the man, though the article goes on to say that his marriage to 'a poor girl without money' had done much to allay suspicions about him.

The publication of the article, on 11th October, alerted those who had long been looking for Hatfield. When the couple returned to Keswick, after their honeymoon in Scotland, the authorities were waiting. He was arrested and charged with defrauding the Post Office by franking his letters as an MP and getting them delivered free. It was a capital offence.

Almost immediately Hatfield escaped and made his way across the mountains. During the manhunt that ensued, the whole country found itself caught up in the fairytale romance that had turned to high drama.

It soon emerged that Hatfield was an experienced confidence trickster who had spent many years in prison. He was a bigamist too. He had been married twice before Mary, and the second wife, with two children, was still alive. Letters came to light from the two abandoned wives, pathetically pleading with him to come back. It was this, the heartless desertion of wife and children, that Coleridge found unforgivable. His articles for the *Morning Post* took on a venomous tone. Hatfield was now 'the Keswick Imposter', 'this atrocious villain'. 'Never surely', Coleridge wrote, 'did an equal number of letters disclose a thicker swarm of villainies .... It is greatly to be hoped that the wretch will be apprehended – a more detestable action was surely never perpetrated.' The writing is unusually inflamed for Coleridge. Perhaps his feelings were intensified by the precarious state of his own marriage. It is odd to reflect that just over a year after writing in these terms, Coleridge himself was to leave for the Mediterranean, also deserting his wife and children, though not in so brutal and total a fashion as Hatfield had done.

Hatfield dodged about England and Wales and was finally recaptured in Brecon. He was taken to London for questioning, then sent to Carlisle for trial. Public interest had risen to fever-pitch, further fuelled by the fact that Mary was now known to be pregnant. To Coleridge's wonder and indignation there were still many in Cumberland, in Keswick and Carlisle especially, who took Hatfield's side.

He was tried in August 1803 and found guilty on three counts of forgery, among them that of signing a false name 'in order to avoid the payment of the duty on postage'. He was sentenced to death by hanging.

Coleridge and the Wordsworths were in Carlisle when the trial reached its climax. They were on their way to a touring holiday in Scotland. A few hours after Hatfield had been condemned, Coleridge visited him.

It is not known why Hatfield agreed to the meeting. Perhaps (though it seems unlikely) he did not know it was Coleridge who had written the article that led to his arrest, and the subsequent pieces calling for his punishment. Perhaps he knew this but desperately hoped he might yet be able to charm his visitor into changing his attitude, and induce him to add his voice to those who were calling for a reprieve. If that was his aim, it was totally unsuccessful. Coleridge wrote only two lines in his *Notebook* about the prison visit:

Then visited Hatfield, impelled by Miss Wordsworth – *vain*, a hypocrite. It is not by mere Thought, I can understand this man.

The words sound dismissive but Coleridge long continued to be haunted by Hatfield. Many years later Thomas De Quincey, writing about the letters from Hatfield's abandoned wives, said: 'Great was the emotion of Coleridge when he recurred to his remembrance of these letters, and bitter – almost vindictive – was the indignation with which he spoke of Hatfield.'

The story was a newspaper sensation in its day and has proved to be of enduring interest. Its themes have a universal appeal – the corruption of young innocence by the scheming sophisticate; the conman's intriguing blend of charm and selfish ruthlessness; the dramatic plunge from all the joys of 'the romantic marriage' to the depths of public disgrace and death; the fact that Hatfield's downfall sprang from a moment of impulsive virtue, when he let his heart rule his head.

Wordsworth gave the story a passing mention in his autobiographical poem 'The Prelude':

> Unfaithful to a virtuous wife,
> Deserted and deceived, the spoiler came ...
> And wooed the artless daughter of the hills
> And wedded her in cruel mockery.

A novel based on the Hatfield story was published in 1848 and another, Philip Lindsay's *Love Rides to Buttermere*, in 1958. Graham Sutton made it the subject of a radio play. And in 1987 Melvyn Bragg found fresh things to reveal in *The Maid of Buttermere*, particularly the strong religious element in Hatfield's complex personality.

It took Mary some time to recover from her ordeal. Her child by Hatfield died in infancy. But four years after Hatfield's hanging she married a Caldbeck farmer. They had four children and lived, by all accounts, in happy harmony. Her grace and charm, her sunny nature and much of her early beauty survived, they say, until her death in 1837.

CHAPTER THREE

To Ennerdale

Buttermere, 9 miles from Keswick, is the halfway point of the first day's walk. I spent an hour in the crowded bar, drying out a little and writing up my notes. My notebook, kept in a plastic wrapper in the inside pocket of my anorak, was dry. The garish lights of a gambling machine against the wall kept up their perpetual, mindless winking. I wondered what Coleridge would have made of that form of entertainment. He was a natural risk-taker but gambling for money had no interest for him, and doing it with an electronic device, with no call for skill or intelligence, would have seemed a strange aberration. Nor would he have approved of the condom dispenser in the men's lavatory.

Occasionally I glanced through the steamed-up windows. It was still raining heartily. When I went to the door and peered out it appeared to be raining harder than ever. A man, addressing no one in particular, said: 'We were going to walk round the lake. Might as well walk into it.'

I put on the anorak, shouldered the soggy rucksack and set off. The way ahead lay due west, straight into the wind and weather.

At first the path leads across level fields, between stone walls, then over a bridge across the river that joins Buttermere to Crummock Water. The ground beyond is usually marshy; now it was running with water.

I was pleased to see that work had been done here to restore and improve the path. A few years before it was a very boggy spot. Now it was possible to walk on stones, firmly set into the ground. This is one of the good things that has happened in the Lake District in the 1980s. They call it 'upland management' in official circles – the business of keeping the paths across the fells as pleasant to walk and as sightly as possible, and protecting the hills from the ravages of erosion.

Before the Second World War, fears were voiced about the damaging effects of increasing numbers of people tramping the fells. Since the war, the problem has grown much more serious, especially on the popular routes. If everyone always walked carefully and in single file all would be well. But fell-walking, although a solitary delight for the few, is regarded by most people as a convivial pursuit. They like to chat along the way, sharing the experience. Some walk clumsily. Others, young men and children usually, race each other downhill. A few years of this means the destruction of the old tracks, and the virtual devastation of the fellside.

The process is straightforward. The passage of too many boots kills the grass and reveals a thin top-soil and pebbles. Heavy rainfall then turns the path into a watercourse, washing out the stones and soil. In the more level sections the ground becomes swampy. In steeper places what was a path turns into a deep gully, covered in loose rubble. Since neither is any pleasure to walk on, people are forced to seek the turf on the side and the same erosive process begins there. So the ugly scars across the mountains grow wider, up to 20 yards across in places and visible from miles away. Some of them can be clearly seen on photographs taken from a satellite nearly 400 miles above.

In the past decade, however, the Lake District Special Planning Board (the planning authority for the 880 square miles of the National Park) and the National Trust (which owns about a quarter of the area) have both organised small working parties to tackle the problem. The results have been remarkable. Crumbling old stiles and gates and bridges have been replaced; and many of the most badly eroded tracks have been rebuilt, using much the same methods as the Romans used nearly 2,000 years ago. For the most part the job has been done sensitively, and the paths have been made to look as natural and unobtrusive as possible. Grass seed has been scattered on the worst-affected places and the land is already recovering. The new paths are built to last. And there seems no good reason, barring a major earthquake, why they should not last for ever.

I was grateful for the work that had been done here, and so were others. Despite the continuing downpour, I passed several parties on the 2 miles to Scale Force. 'Force' is the local name for a waterfall, derived from the Norse *fors*. There are many fine waterfalls in the Lake District, and Scale Force is among the most impressive. It claims the longest sheer drop in the District, variously estimated at between 100 and 125 feet. In spate, it is a wild and stirring spectacle. It was a tourist attraction before Coleridge's time.

Captain Joseph Budworth was taken to view it in 1792. He found the path 'very uneven and boggy' but was thrilled by what he saw:

> Scale-Force Waterfall is 200 feet perpendicular, except where it flushes over a small jut; the steep on both sides is covered with variety of moss, fern, ash and oak, all fed by the constant spray and flourish in indescribable verdure; the delicacy of the effect is heightened by being in a narrow chasm, a hundred yards in the rock, before it rushes into the lower fall, at the point of which you have the grand view: clamber up the left side and look into the first basin, and although you may be wet with the spray, you cannot help feeling the solemnity of this deep, this musical abyss, enchanting as verdure and melody can make it ....

Coleridge, too, went to see the fall on his first visit to the Lake District, in November 1799, and wrote in his *Notebook*:

> The first fall is a thin broad white ribbon from a stupendous Height, uninterrupted tho' not unimpinged by, the perpendicular Rock down which it falls ... there is no pool at the bottom, but a common shallow brook over small flattish pebbles – but the chasm thro' which it flows is stupendous – so wildly wooded that the mosses and wet weeds and perilous Tree increase the Horror of the rocks which *ledge* only enough to interrupt not stop your fall – and the Tree – O God! to think of a poor Wretch hanging with one arm from it .... I never saw Trees on rock Zigzag in

their Lines more beautifully – Trees white in bark and more than half over patched with blackish Moss – Then the green moss upon the rocks mingled with flats and little precipices of the grey Rock – and Trees again.

A rough series of steps had been chipped in the rock – by Joseph Robinson, father of 'the Beauty of Buttermere' – to enable the more daring tourists to ascend a little way up the side of the falling water. In Victorian times, and in the first two decades of this century, visitors holidaying in the Keswick area would make a trip to Scale Force the climax of a day-long excursion which was called 'the Buttermere round'. They rode, in coaches pulled by four horses, along the Borrowdale Valley; up to the top of Honister Pass to see the slate-quarrying; then steeply down the other side and along the shores of the lake to Buttermere village. There were three hotels there then – the Fish, the Victoria (which is now called the Bridge), and the Buttermere Hotel (which is now a youth hostel). The tourists would lunch at one of the hotels, walk across the fields to Crummock Water and pay a shilling to have themselves rowed across the lake. The boatman would then wait while they went up the hill to admire the waterfall.

In the 1920s there were wooden steps from the foot of the fall to the ledge at the bottom of the big drop. The *Ward Lock Guide* for 1927 advises people to ignore them; there had, it seems, been a fatal accident there, caused by a falling rock. Some time later these steps were removed, but in the summer of 1959 a new wooden ladder was installed by a National Trust woodman called Kendall Vickers. Although he made a sturdy job of it, it was once again the scene of accidents, none of them fatal but serious enough. The National Trust had the ladder removed at the end of the 1960s and since then those who want to gain the ledge have had to clamber up as Captain Budworth did two centuries ago. It is usually slimy.

It was very slimy when I got there so I did not attempt the climb. The fall was in magnificent trim, full and powerful, thundering down the long drop in a wide white sheet that seemed almost solid, then breaking up to roar and foam through the gully below. The dark rock and vegetation on the side walls glistened with moisture. The sound of the water filled my ears, and some quality of the light made the abundant red berries of the mountain ash glow and sparkle with a vividness I had not seen before.

On the occasion of Coleridge's second visit to Scale Force the fall was not in a particularly lively condition. He gave it no more than a passing but vivid mention in his letter to Sara Hutchinson:

> ... passed by Scale Force, the white downfall of which glimmered thro' the Trees, that hang before it like bushy Hair over a madman's Eyes ...

Coleridge loved water in all its natural states – ice and the ocean, lakes and rivers, fountains and waterfalls. Water images recur in his poems. 'Kubla Khan', for example, in its brief 56 lines, includes a 'sacred river', 'a sunless sea', 'sinuous rills', 'a mighty fountain', 'a lifeless ocean' and 'caves of ice'. His *Notebooks* contain many detailed descriptions of waterfalls, comparing their characters and finding a metaphysical significance in them – the matter constantly changing while the overall shape and pattern remain constant: he saw this as 'an awful Image and Shadow of God and the World'. And in one of his philosophical articles he uses the idea of a mountain spring freezing and thawing to illustrate the way truth patiently finds its way:

> Truth considered in itself and in the effects natural to it, may be conceived as a gentle spring of water-source, warm from the genial earth, and breathing up into the snow drift that is piled over and around its outlet. It turns the obstacle into its own form and character, and as it makes its way increases its stream. And should it be arrested in its course by a chilling season, it suffers delay, not loss, and waits only for a change in the wind to awaken and again roll onwards.

This passage must have been at the back of Wordsworth's mind many years later when, writing of his friend's death, he spoke of the moment when

... every mortal power of Coleridge
Was frozen at its marvellous source.

Wordsworth undoubtedly shared his friend's passion for moving water. The opening lines of his first version of 'The Prelude' describe how the River Derwent, running past his first home

... sent a voice
That flowed along my dreams ...
Make ceaseless music through the night and day,
Which with its steady cadence tempering
Our human waywardness, composed my thoughts
To more than infant softness, giving me
Among the fretful dwellings of mankind
A knowledge, a dim earnest, of the calm
Which Nature breathes among the fields and groves.

Much later he wrote 34 sonnets celebrating the varied scenes as you follow the progress of the River Duddon from its source high up on Wrynose Fell to the Irish Sea.

It is often said that the sound of running water is the only noise we can hear endlessly without becoming irritated. (Even the voice of a loved one can grow tiresome after a few hours.) The reasons are, I believe, rooted in our origins. After all, we spend the first nine months of our existence inside the mother's womb, listening to the continuous gurglings of her body juices all around us, and it is bound to be consoling and cheering to be reminded, however subconsciously, of those blissful days when we were warm and safe and never called upon to do anything at all. Even more atavistically, we all derive, the evolutionists tell us, from sea creatures that adapted to life on dry land.

There was no lack of water as I pushed on beyond Scale Force. The ground rises steadily, with little in the way of distinguishing features. There was no path there in 1802 and, although the modern maps indicate a path, it is easily missed. Visibility was poor and getting worse. To my left, I knew, rose the steep slopes of Red Pike, which Thomas West called 'the ferruginous mountain', but they were swathed in swirling mist. My spectacles were running with rainwater on the outside and steamed up on the inside, and I no longer had anything I could dry them with. I soon found myself wading through peaty bogs, struggling up slippery grass, leaping across gullies that had become torrents. The only variation in the weather came when a thunderstorm moved across, close overhead. I began to feel increasingly like King Lear in the storm on the heath. It was the only time, in the nine days of the walk, when I felt tempted to abandon the whole thing.

This area is not, in good conditions, a particularly appealing one. Even Wainwright found no redeeming charms:

> If walkers were called upon to vote for the Lakeland pass they considered least attractive, there is little doubt that Floutern Pass would top the poll with a thumping majority ... the intermediate stages are without charm or beauty and contain an extensive quagmire ... Nor have the surrounding fells any visual appeal: they are barren, lack character, are without features of interest, undistinguished in outline and share in the general hopelessness of the landscape ... Floutern, frankly, is a mess.

Coleridge was not so dismissive of Floutern Pass. His spirits remained buoyant as he marched uphill, stopping frequently to make notes. This part of the walk, above Scale Force, shows how he used his notes when composing his letter. In the *Notebook* he wrote:

> ... gain a level – mossy soft ground, every man his own path-maker – skip and jump – where rushes grow, a man may go – Red Pike peeps in on you upon your left ... you cross the pretty Beck that goes to Loweswater – you again ascend a ruined sheep fold –

here I write these lines, a wild green view, bleating of
Sheep and noise of waters ...

He clearly had the book open before him when he sat
down, a day or two later, to write to Sara:

... and climbed till I gained the first Level – here it
was 'every man his own path-maker', and I went
directly cross it – upon soft mossy Ground, with many
a hop, skip and jump, and many an occasion for
observing the Truth of the old Saying: where Rushes
grow, a Man may go. Red Pike, a dolphin-shaped Peak
of a deep red, looked in upon me from over the Fell
on my Left .... Again I reached an ascent, climbed
up, and came to a ruined Sheepfold – a wild green
view all around me, bleating of Sheep and noise of
waters – I sate there near 20 minutes, the Sun setting
on the hill behind with a soft watery gleam ... I left
the Sheepfold with regret – for of all things a ruined
Sheepfold in a desolate place is the dearest to me, and
fills me most with Dreams and Visions and tender
thoughts of those I love best.

The one he loved best was undoubtedly Sara Hutchinson,
but he must also have been thinking, at this moment, of Wordsworth and particularly of the narrative poem 'Michael' that
Wordsworth had written in 1800. It tells the story of an old
Grasmere shepherd who, faced with a heavy debt, agrees to send
his beloved son to a job in the city, in the hope that he will help
pay off the debt. The evening before the son's departure Michael
takes him 'Up the tumultuous brook of Greenhead Ghyll' to the
spot where he plans to build a sheepfold. He gets the boy to set
the first cornerstone in place. The outcome is in Wordsworth's
gloomiest manner – the son falls prey to the temptations of the
city – but the uncompleted sheepfold stands as a symbol of
parental loyalty and rustic patience and endurance. Coleridge
found it very telling. It was read to him by the author soon after
its composition, and Coleridge wrote about it to Humphry
Davy:

It is of a mild, unimposing character; but full of beauties to those short-necked men who have their hearts sufficiently near their heads ... Believe me, that such scenes and such characters really exist in this county – the superiority of the small Estatesman, such as Wordsworth paints in old Michael, is a God compared to our Peasants and small farmers in the South; and furnishes important documents of the kindly ministrations of local attachment and hereditary descent ...

The sheepfold on Floutern Pass can still be seen, presumably a little more ruined than it was in 1802 but still recognisable.

By the time Coleridge tore himself away from the spot, the sun had dropped behind the hill ahead. He pressed on, admiring 'a frightful craggy precipice with shivers, and all wrinkled' ['shivers' were screes], to reach the sedgy plateau that holds Floutern Tarn. There is a minor puzzle here. In both his *Notebook* and his letter Coleridge describes the tarn as 'about 100 yards in length, and not more than 7 or 8 in breadth'. It is certainly long and narrow, but it is nothing like so narrow as that today. At its thinnest point it is more than twice the breadth he gave it. Have the waters of the tarn grown wider in the intervening years? Or did Coleridge, who was generally fairly accurate in his reckoning, simply get it wrong?

The summit of the pass is just above the tarn, and when he got there Coleridge could see the declining sun again. He stopped to survey the view all round:

I never saw a more heart-raising Scene. I turned and looked on the Scene which I had left behind, a marvellous group of mountains, wonderfully and admirably arranged – not a single minute object to interrupt the oneness of the view, excepting those two green Fields in Buttermere – but before me the glorious Sea with the high Coast and Mountains of the Isle of Mann, perfectly distinct – and three Ships in view.

This is from the letter to Sara. In his *Notebook* he added a revealing aside: '... what a scene for Salvator Rosa'. Rosa, an Italian painter, was much admired for the savagery and sublimity of his landscapes. Despite his contempt for the 'picturesque' tourists, Coleridge was sufficiently a child of his time to think of the fells, perhaps in an unguarded moment, in terms of oil painting.

Coleridge did not know – no one knew it then – that the route he had been following is one of special geological interest, running roughly along the junction of two completely different rock formations.

On his right-hand side, to the north, lay the smooth-sloped mountains, composed of what is now called Skiddaw Slate. Coleridge had seen them as a giants' encampment. Melvyn Bragg describes the northern fells as an area 'where a gentle herd of gigantic and ancient elephants seem to have lain down to sleep, their wrinkled hides lightly blanketed with bracken'. This slaty, friable rock is certainly ancient. The geologists say it is several thousands of feet in depth and was formed, over millions of years, when the region was covered by a shallow sea. This started, they say, some 500 million years ago or more.

On his other side, the mountains to the south are of Borrowdale Volcanic rock, created at a much later period by violent underwater eruptions. They are more dramatic in appearance, craggy and jagged and inclined to the vertical. These are the places frequented by rock-climbers.

The Lake District includes other kinds of strata too, and there is much complex intermingling and overlapping. The whole structure was eroded and moulded, over countless millennia, by various forces – shifts in the earth's crust, wind and rain, frost and ice. The present outlines were carved out by receding, melting glaciers at the end of the last great Ice Age, a mere matter of 10,000 to 20,000 years ago. Floutern Pass was formed in this way, and you can see the evidence in the valley bottom – smooth-backed humps of glacial drift, now overgrown with grasses and bracken.

Little of this was known at the beginning of the nineteenth century. A few people, Coleridge among them, had noticed that the mountain shapes, the colour and texture of the rock as well, varied from area to area. But no one knew how it had come about. Most people accepted the Genesis story that the whole universe had been created by God in six days. They believed he had done it (the calculations were based on a thorough study of Old Testament chronology) some 6,000 years ago. Puzzling phenomena like banks of moraine and isolated boulders in the valley bottoms were thought to have been left behind by the subsiding waters of Noah's Flood.

The man who pioneered the understanding of Lakeland geology was living in Keswick when Coleridge lived there. Jonathan Otley had moved to the town from Grasmere to set up in business as a weaver of swill baskets (heavy-duty baskets made out of wood shavings). But he was practical and enterprising, and quickly branched out into other trades – engraving and the repair of all kinds of machinery, especially clocks and watches. He was a good workman, reliable and honest, and soon won widespread respect. The population of Keswick was just over 1,000 at that time (it is now five times bigger), so it is possible that he met Coleridge, though there is no evidence for this. Coleridge would certainly have been impressed by the man, his powerful natural intelligence, his acute observation, his determined pursuit of knowledge, the range of his interests – botany and meteorology and geology. Otley lived at a time when it was still possible for such a man, however lacking in formal education, to contribute to scientific advance. His contribution was considerable.

In the *Lonsdale Magazine* for 1820 he published a letter entitled 'The threefold division of the rocks of the Lake District'. The rocks were Skiddaw Slate in the north, Borrowdale Volcanic in the centre, and Silurian Slate in the south. He expanded the letter into a full-length article which he included in a guidebook, *A Concise Description of the English Lakes*, published in 1823. That same year he was visited by Adam Sedgwick, Professor of Geology at Trinity College, Cambridge. Otley took Sedgwick into the hills, showed his discoveries and explained his theories. They became lifelong friends, and it was through Sedgwick that Otley's ideas proved influential in the emergent science of geology.

Had Coleridge known, in August 1802, how the mountains he was walking across had been created, he would have been fascinated. He took a keen, though amateur, interest in scientific advances. He had great respect for the brilliant young scientist Humphry Davy (who became a Professor of Chemistry at the Royal Institution in 1802) and his letters to Davy are among his liveliest, sparkling with ideas and jokes, full of requests for information and advice about electricity and galvanism and chemical experiments he could do. 'I shall attack chemistry', he promised, 'like a Shark.' He was too impractical to make much of any experiments but retained his appetite for fresh discoveries, especially when they could be related to his continuing search for the unity of creation. He loved the idea of immensity. To be told that the planet earth was the product, not of six days' hard labour by God, but of the violent interplay of prodigious natural forces over hundreds of millions of years would have appealed enormously to his imagination.

It would have disturbed him too. He was a dedicated Christian. The Bible's representation of man as the central purpose of the universe, created in God's image and redeemed by his son, had long been undermined by one branch of scientific inquiry, astronomy. Throughout the eighteenth century there had been further assaults on the faith from doubters and rationalists of varying persuasions – deists, agnostics, atheists and others. As the century advanced the pressure mounted, and it was maintained in the nineteenth century, first by the geologists, then the biologists. We can only guess what Coleridge's reaction to all this would have been. He had, I think, too high a regard for scientific method to take the fundamentalist line that whatever contradicted the word of God as revealed in the Bible must be wrong and wicked. I suspect that he would have been foremost among those who worked to find ways of reconciling the new knowledge with the old faith.

The summit of Floutern Pass is just over 1,000 feet above sea level. But the panoramic view that Coleridge surveyed was completely hidden from me by the unabating storm. I could see no more than a few yards of the path ahead and a recently installed wire fence alongside it. These fences are among the more obvious ways in which the appearance of the fells has changed in two centuries. Now, when a farmer wishes to mark his boundaries, or stop his sheep from straying on to dangerous ground, he throws a load of wooden stakes and some rolls of wire into the back of his four-wheel-drive vehicle and goes off, with an assistant, to do the job quickly and cheaply.

In Coleridge's day the boundaries were marked much more laboriously and slowly – by building dry-stone walls. The sight of these walls, snaking their way up and across the steep hillsides, is still guaranteed to impress newcomers to the Lake District. Most of them were built between 1750 and 1850 by gangs of itinerant labourers who often bivouacked on the fellside to spare themselves the long trudge to work each morning. According to one surviving set of accounts, a gang was paid one shilling and sixpence for every $7\frac{1}{2}$ yards of wall. True to its name, the dry-stone wall is held together not by mortar or cement but by its cunning construction. It consists of two parallel walls, each some $5\frac{1}{2}$ feet high, leaning together and linked by larger rocks known as 'through-stones'. The walls had to withstand the ravages of wind and rain, heavy frosts and deep snowfalls, shifts and slips of the earth. They did. Indeed, most of them stand their ground to this day.

It was dusk as Coleridge dropped down towards Ennerdale but there was enough light for him to see across the lake to Anglers' Crag:

> On the opposite Shore in the middle and narrow part of the Lake there bulges out a huge Crag, called angling Stone, being a famous station for anglers – and the reflection of this Crag in the Water is admirable – pillars or rather it looks like the pipes of some enormous Organ in a rich golden Color.

Though it was much earlier in the day when I descended into Ennerdale Valley, I saw none of this. My notes record nothing more than a series of rather severely worded notices by the path:

> Keep your dog under strict control.

Keep to the path and keep your dog on the lead.
Private property. Access to Floutern Tarn.

Most dogs have an instinctive urge to move sheep about, and this is a matter of great concern to the fell farmers, especially in lambing time in early spring. 'We can strive to cure or prevent most ailments that our sheep get,' a fell shepherd said recently, 'but there's yan thing we canna' cure and there's yan thing we canna' prevent – and that's visitors and bloody dogs. They cause biggest losses of our sheep.' Some farms put out notices saying 'Number of dogs shot to date – 12', almost certainly exaggerating the number of executions. But the lambs are the shepherd's livelihood and he has the legal right, if he thinks his flocks are threatened, to shoot the offending dog.

At last I reached the valley road. In the 6 miles from Scale Force I had not seen anyone. It was hardly surprising. It is not a much-frequented route at the best of times, and this was far from being the best. The rain continued to beat into my face as I plodded the last mile of tarmac lane to Ennerdale Bridge.

Coleridge went through the village and up the hill beyond to spend the night at John Ponsonby's farm at Long Moor. I had had enough for one day, however, and set about looking for somewhere to stay. As I had feared, it was not easy.

Ennerdale Bridge is a small village and by the time I arrived, at 5.30 p.m., all the available accommodation had been taken by 'coast-to-coast' walkers. People could not have been more helpful but there was simply no room left. Everyone expressed regret and suggested another address. I do not know how many doors I knocked on until, close to despair, I went to the back door of the pub, the Fox and Hounds, vaguely hoping they might let me unroll my mattress on the bar floor after closing time.

The pub was not yet open but I was invited in, made to sit down, and given a mug of tea to drink while the landlady phoned round on my behalf. It was a long time before she struck lucky. But then she rang Mrs Arlene Robson, who had just arrived home with her family from a holiday in Spain and who, in consequence, had not been planning to let out her spare room quite so quickly. Presumably a moving account of my condition was given. Mrs Robson relented. I was told the good news and then, most heart-warming of all, the landlord insisted on driving me to the Robsons' house in his car, though it was not a quarter of a mile away.

The Robsons made me welcome. I was shown to a neat little upstairs room at the front of the house where there was a fire. Mrs Robson brought me tea and biscuits and a towel and told me to get all my wet clothes off and hand them over to be dried overnight. Suddenly the world seemed a better, friendlier place.

I went back to the pub later on for a couple of pints of Theakston's best bitter and a plate of Cumberland sausage and black pudding and chips. I let the warmth and comfort enfold me. The place was full of cheery ramblers, most of them comparing notes about the day's weather. A local woman said she could not recall such a downpour. She reckoned 3 inches had fallen.

'It wouldn't surprise me,' I said with feeling. 'I suppose we needed it.'

'Not like that,' she replied severely.

Later I asked the barman if there was anyone in the area by the name of Ponsonby.

'Yes,' he said. 'Two brothers. They live next door to each other, at the top of the hill, on the way to Long Moor.'

'Would they be related, do you think, to a man called John Ponsonby who ran Long Moor farm 200 years ago?'

'Could be. I think I've heard something of that. But it were long since.'

He told me exactly where the brothers lived and I decided I would go and see them next morning.

The rain was beginning to ease off as I walked back to Mrs Robson's.

CHAPTER FOUR

Ennerdale and the Environment

Waking early next morning, I saw that the sky was clear and bright. I stayed in bed, luxuriously reading for another hour, then turned on the television for the weather forecast. The next few days were going to be changeable.

Downstairs I confronted the formidable breakfast that I was to find standard fare on the bed and breakfast circuit: cornflakes; bacon, eggs, sausage, fried tomatoes and fried bread; unlimited toast and marmalade; a big pot of tea. For this and the night's lodging and the drying of my clothes I was charged £10.

Over breakfast I looked through the local paper, the *Whitehaven News*, which serves the industrial coastlands of Cumbria. The main story was about gangs of unemployed teenagers on a council estate who had been sniffing glue, slashing themselves and terrifying elderly neighbours. But the paper's over-riding preoccupation was with environmental issues. A Workington firm had been fined for polluting a stream. The Water Authority was contesting claims made by Friends of the Earth that Cumbria's drinking water was being poisoned by excessive amounts of lead and aluminium. The general manager of Marchon, the chemical works at Whitehaven, said he and his fellow-directors were as concerned as anyone else about recent accidental emissions and were doing all they could to prevent any recurrence. Greenpeace activists were about to renew their campaign against the discharge of radioactive material into the Irish Sea by the nuclear plant at Sellafield. British Nuclear Fuels had bought two pages of the paper to reassure the public that they were doing everything possible to keep to a minimum all health hazards that might arise from the Sellafield operations.

In Coleridge's day the coast of West Cumberland was riding

a wave of industrial and mercantile prosperity. The region held rich seams of coal and iron. There were blast furnaces and foundries and many mills, and scores of ancilliary enterprises and trades. Whitehaven was one of England's leading ports, despatching coal to Ireland, receiving tobacco and rum and much else from across the Atlantic. It was a bustling place and Whitehaven itself was a handsome, planned, Georgian town, with capacious warehouses and shipyards, and factories making rope and sails. Two centuries later all these things are dead and gone, replaced by new kinds of industrial enterprise. It cannot possibly have occurred to anyone then that man's mastery of physics and chemistry and technology would one day reach the point where it would seem to threaten his continued existence. Oddly enough, the enterprise that most people see as presenting the greatest threat, the nuclear complex at Sellafield, has done more than anything else to sustain the region. It employs, directly or indirectly, some 14,000 people, and it has spent more than £3 million restoring the Georgian terraces of Whitehaven to their pristine splendour.

Coleridge's first night away from home was spent at Long Moor Farm as the guest of Mr John Ponsonby who gave him, Coleridge says, 'a very hearty welcome'. Next morning Mr Ponsonby showed his guest round the area. In the afternoon Coleridge walked to St Bees on the coast, 10 miles or so of comparatively level going.

After breakfast I took my leave of Mrs Robson and walked up the hill towards Long Moor, hoping for a chat with Mr Ponsonby's descendants, if such they were. The two houses were easy to find. They stand together, isolated, by the road that leads to Cold Fell, looking across 200 yards of rough, marshy ground towards Long Moor.

Mr Gordon Ponsonby was at home, sitting before the television in his little front room, contentedly smoking a pipe. He invited me in, turned the volume down and confirmed that he and his brother John, who lived next door, were descended from the Ponsonbys who farmed Long Moor. He was not sure how many generations separated them from Coleridge's host. He had heard of Coleridge but did not know he had once spent the night there. It was over 100 years, he said, since his grandfather had sold the place.

Gordon Ponsonby is a quiet, gentle-mannered man. He was born and brought up in the house where he still lives. After leaving school in the mid-1930s he worked for a few years as a farm labourer but did not enjoy it: 'It was very hard work in those days.' Then he worked for the Forestry Commission in Ennerdale for a couple of years. The Second World War showed him something of the world beyond Cumberland. He was a Royal Marine and went to Egypt and the Lebanon, Sicily and Italy, even Iceland. After the war he came home to work as a lorry-driver, then in a toffee factory in Egremont for 30 years. When the factory closed down in 1985 he retired. He never married.

For the past 17 years his younger brother John has lived next door. John married and had two daughters and is now a widower, working for a paper-packaging firm in Whitehaven.

They have not moved far from the ancestral home. From their front windows they can look across to Long Moor Farm, a long, low, white-fronted stone building, with a distinctive arched window in the middle and the kind of chimneys – square-based and circular above – which Wordsworth recommended. It was built for John Ponsonby in 1792. It was a working farm, sheep mostly, until the mid-1980s. Now the fields have been sold off and the place has been divided into two private houses. Modern extensions have been added at the back where there is a fine old barn. A notice on the gate warns of 'Ciraso Afghans' and, sure enough, as you approach, two large, long-haired dogs bark crossly and rear up at the fencing. Looking to the west you can see, 5 miles away, the factory chimneys of Whitehaven, and the sea beyond.

In his letter to Sara Hutchinson, Coleridge described his welcome by John Ponsonby and went on:

> ... here I stayed the night and the greater part of Monday – the old man went to the head of the Lake with me – the mountains at the head of this Lake and Wast-dale are the Monsters of the Country, bare bleak

Heads, evermore doing deeds of Darkness, weather-plots and storm-conspiracies in the Clouds....

There is a fuller account in the *Notebook*. It is clear that Mr Ponsonby was telling him the names of all the mountains and Coleridge was noting them down and trying to fix their relative positions. The old gentleman was also recounting hunting tales and bits of local lore and gossip. Coleridge scribbled them down in outline – and sometimes obscure – form, presumably hoping to use them as *aides-memoires*:

... under Barter Crag the famous Bield [an animal's den or shelter] of Foxes, 5 cubs – 80 Lambs, Geese, Hares, Mice, Moles, Frogs, dogs –

... Iron Crag – back of this the wild Cat fell into the water, four Hounds and a Terrier with it – when they came up, they were all of a mat, each hold of the Cat – the Cat of all of them – 5 minutes under the water –

... 38 hours without food by the Fox's Bield – because the 2 Foxes would have taken away their young Tod, a Fox

... Fox (last killed) just in Bowness tumbled off the Crags, and broke his hind back – Old Man, in the house, bedrid, heard the hounds – and got up and out – fox trailing his back, and fighting – old man got him before the hunters –

... Bowness the finest piece of savage rock-work I ever saw – great bulging bullsheads of Crag with streams of Shiver [scree] –

... Sheep clinging like Flies to a Grass –

... The Drunkenness of the Ennerdale Priest – item of the Wasdale Priest – item Borrowdale – item Grasmere – Sick at heart – and desperate – poor creatures! The difference of a man in company meeting you on the road, insulting etc. – and meeting you alone – it is then your good esteem only that he can gain – how much milder and more civil.

Ennerdale Noted compleatly fiddle shaped ...

The Bowness he speaks of is Bowness Knott, the crag on the north-eastern side of Ennerdale Water. His list of Lake District parsons who had been driven to the bottle by the remoteness of their situations, and the absence of enlivening company, is sad but not surprising. In fact, the rector of Grasmere was insane and it was his curate, Edward Rowlandson, who was the drunkard. Dorothy Wordsworth had seen him officiating at a funeral in the summer of 1800 and noted reprovingly that 'he did not look as a man ought to on such an occasion'.

I followed Coleridge and made my way to the foot of the lake, $1\frac{1}{2}$ miles from the village. Several parties of coast-to-coasters were going the same way, heading for Black Sail and Honister Pass and Borrowdale. All had brightly coloured anoraks and bulging rucksacks; most were carrying waterproof map-cases and Wainwright's guidebook. Two cheerful young women from the Midlands told me they had already abandoned their boyfriends, defeated by blisters and rain on the first day.

A tarmac lane leads to the lake. On either side the hedgerows were luxuriant and lovely, all growing things washed and freshened by the previous day's long-awaited rain. There were birch, beech and alder; rowan with their shining red berries; a profusion of intertwining blackberries, their fruit almost ripe. The ground was carpeted with grasses and wild flowers in a lively variety of colours – every gradation of green, white and off-white, mustard and the bright yellows of buttercups and dandelion, purples and a romantic misty blue. I can remember no Lakeland summer that compares with that of 1989 for natural abundance. Everything seemed to flourish. Possibly it was the result of a mild and wet winter, followed by many weeks of cloudless skies and sunshine.

Beyond the hedgerows, however, lay a sadder scene – the widespread desolation where rows of mature conifers had lately been felled and dragged away, leaving their stumps showing and the marshy ground littered with pale thin branches. In the distance a group of spruce, as yet untouched by the chainsaw, seemed to be leaning forlornly together.

Ennerdale is one of the remotest and wildest and grandest of the Lake District valleys, its lake bounded on three sides by high mountains: Great Gable at its head; Pillar Mountain and Pillar Rock, the playground of the pioneer rock-climbers, on one side; on the other the high, undulating ridge that divides Ennerdale from Buttermere. Today, however, it is also one of the most damaged valleys of the District. Its slopes, up to the 1,000-foot contour, have been blanketed with conifers by the Forestry Commission, and water is extracted from the lake to supply the factories in and around Whitehaven.

You see evidence of the latter as you approach the lake shore. The River Ehen is channelled between high stone walls. There is a weir. There is a stone-built treatment works. And there are prohibitory notices:

> No swimming or boating.
> No admittance.
> Danger. Chlorine.
> Keep clear. Pumping in operation.

When I arrived at the lakeside in August 1989 I found the level ground crowded with vehicles and machinery of the North-West Water Authority. They had been there for over a month, pumping water out of the lake to keep the supply to Whitehaven flowing. The long dry summer had lowered the surface of the lake until it was well below the level of the weir. At the low point it was almost 5 feet below. But the great downpour of the previous day had solved the problem at a stroke. Ennerdale lake has a large catchment area and its level rises fast after rain. When I arrived it was only 12 inches from the top of the weir and still rising. Before long, the workmen assured me, it would be flowing naturally again. They were packing up and pulling out.

The extraction of water from this lake is on a fairly modest scale and it would be exaggerating to say it does great visual harm in normal circumstances. But it becomes very unsightly after long periods without rain. Then the level drops to reveal arid stretches of mud and stone, creating an unnatural and very obvious white rim all round the water's edge. Unfortunately such periods seem to be occurring more frequently nowadays.

Things would certainly have been very much worse here,

and at Wastwater, had it not been for a major victory won by the environmentalists a few years before.

In the spring of 1978 the North-West Water Authority (then a government body, now a private company) announced their intention to get more water out of Ennerdale through raising its level by 4 feet. It would have meant a much higher weir; a long and obtrusive embankment; some re-routing of the river; the loss of many acres of farming land. Within the National Park, all building proposals (right down to putting a porch on your front door) go to the Special Planning Board for approval. They are currently refusing over 20 per cent of applications, which goes a long way towards explaining their unpopularity. They rejected this one firmly.

The issue was further complicated in early 1979, when British Nuclear Fuels said they needed to take much more water, three times more than currently, out of Wastwater. They wanted this water because it was exceptionally pure and would save them a lot of money in processing and purifying. The Water Authority opposed this idea because, they said, they had accounted for Sellafield's needs in their plans for Ennerdale.

It was decided that the whole matter should be determined by a public inquiry, presided over by the Inspector, Mr D. H. Komlosy. This took place in Whitehaven between mid-January and early May 1980.

The heartening thing about what happened next was the way in which the many interested parties worked together towards a common end. The Special Planning Board is the overall authority for the National Park region but it is not the only one. There is Cumbria County Council, the District Councils, town and parish councils, each with their own interests to protect. There is the Water Authority and the Forestry Commission. The National Trust is by far the biggest landowner. Many national organisations keep an anxious eye on the Lake District: the Countryside Commission, the Council for the Protection of Rural England, Friends of the Earth, the Country Landowners' Association, the National Farmers' Union. And there are numerous special interest groups – for ramblers and mountaineers, naturalists and anglers, caravanners and youthhostellers and others, all with national and regional organisations. Their interests are not identical and too often in the past, when some environmental threat has arisen, they have been divided – campaigning separately, confusing the issues, undermining each other's arguments.

This was not allowed to happen in the 1980 battle for the two lakes. And most of the credit for this goes to one vital group not yet mentioned, the Friends of the Lake District, formed in 1934 'to organise concerted action for protecting the landscape and natural beauty of the Lake District'.

As early as April 1978 the Friends set up a Save Ennerdale Campaign Committee, embracing most of the groups who opposed the Water Authority's plan. When they heard that Wastwater was also threatened the Committee broadened its base to fight both causes. It discovered that the extra water required could be taken from near the mouth of the River Derwent at Workington, with no damage to the environment, at an extra cost of under £5 million. Two leaflets were printed – 'Save Ennerdale' and 'Defend Wastwater'. They got extensive and favourable publicity in the national newspapers and on television. The Friends began to collect money to pay their legal costs at the public inquiry.

The whole campaign was orchestrated by Geoffrey Berry of Kendal, a gentle-mannered man of great charm but a formidable campaigner. He had fought many environmentalist battles. He was Secretary of the Friends from 1966 to 1976, and after that their Consultant Secretary. He was a qualified chartered accountant with experience in local government and administration; he loved hill-walking and the landscape of northern England; he was a good, clear writer and a superb photographer; a man of persuasive powers, he devoted them, with selfless dedication, to the conservation cause.

The inquiry sat for 57 days and heard two and a half million words of argument and counter-argument. When the sittings concluded, the Inspector went to look at the relevant sites. Visiting Ennerdale, in June 1980, he found that the lake level had sunk below the weir and 20 diesel pumps were noisily forcing the water over the barrier.

The Inspector's report went to the Secretary of State for the Environment in the summer of 1981. Just before Christmas the then Minister, Mr Michael Heseltine, announced that, on the Inspector's recommendation, he had decided to reject the plans for both lakes. The Inspector had found them unacceptable on environmental grounds. About Ennerdale the Inspector said:

> This lake is situated in a very special part of the Lake District National Park. I therefore consider the proposed works which had been stated as being required for raising the lake, not only involving substantial building, but remodelling a large part of the northerly shore, would be totally out of keeping with such a scene.

It was a famous victory. The conservationists' cause had been helped by the fact that their two opponents, the Water Authority and British Nuclear Fuels, were arguing different cases. Fundamentally, though, it was not the disarray of the enemy that determined the issue but the level-headed and united manner in which the environmentalists had operated. Geoffrey Berry wrote a little book about it, *A Tale of Two Lakes* (Friends of the Lake District, 1982). He died, still hard at work for the conservation cause, in January 1988.

The victory was all the sweeter because the cause had suffered a very serious setback nine years before. In 1972 a public inquiry sanctioned the building of a fast motor road across the northern Lake District, linking the M6 motorway at Penrith with the industries of West Cumbria. The environmentalists fought against it but they were defeated by a combination of business interests and successive governments (first Labour, then Conservative) who were more concerned with short-term economic palliatives than the long-term damage to the National Park. The result was the A66, a brutal and ugly gash across once-lovely countryside. A vast viaduct was thrown across the River Greta, Coleridge's river, near Keswick. The winding, tree-lined lane by the western shore of Bassenthwaite Lake became a dual carriageway and many trees and shrubs were destroyed.

Now, even on the summit of Blencathra, you can see and hear the fast-moving traffic rumbling endlessly along, more than 2,000 feet below. The scheme was bulldozed through, with a good deal of official chicanery, despite the fact that there was a perfectly acceptable alternative route a few miles to the north and outside the National Park which would have cost just over £1 million more to construct. The damage done was irreparable.

A decade later Ennerdale Lake was spared such a fate, though above the lake, the river bank and the lower slopes of the fells on either side, over a stretch of more than 5 miles, have been covered with Forestry Commission conifers. None of the valleys that Coleridge visited on his walk has been more completely transformed than Ennerdale.

Afforestation is among the oldest of the Lake District's afflictions. It had already started before Coleridge went to live in Keswick. In the 1790s the notorious Bishop Watson of Llandaff, who held many lucrative church offices and attended to none of them, was planting extensive larch woods along the shores of Windermere. Similar plantations soon appeared above the waters of Derwentwater and Bassenthwaite Lake. It was partly for profit, partly because some people thought them attractive. Others thought them repulsive, and among the disapprovers none was more ferociously articulate than Wordsworth, who condemned the larch in his *Guide to the Lakes*:

> ... as a tree, it is less than any other pleasing; its branches (for *boughs* it has none) have no variety in the youth of the tree, and little dignity, even when it attains its full growth; *leaves* it cannot be said to have, consequently neither affords shade nor shelter. In spring the larch becomes green long before the native trees; and its green is so peculiar and vivid, that finding nothing to harmonize with it, wherever it comes forth, a disagreeable speck is produced. In summer, when all other trees are in their pride, it is of a dingy lifeless hue; in autumn of a spiritless unvaried yellow, and in winter it is still more lamentably distinguished from every other deciduous tree of the forest, for they

seem only to sleep, but the larch appears absolutely dead.

So much for the individual larch. Wordsworth went on to condemn the way it was being planted en masse: '... ten thousand of this spiky tree, the larch, are stuck in at once upon the side of a hill: they can grow into nothing but deformity'. It is almost frightening to contemplate what the poet would have said if he could have seen Ennerdale today.

The first extensive afforestation in the district took place shortly before the First World War, when Manchester won its fight to make Thirlmere a reservoir and planted nearly 2,000 acres of the land around the lake with conifers, set close together in straight lines. The primary aim was to protect the catchment area from erosion. The secondary one was profit from timber, for these are fast-growing trees. The planted area was securely fenced to keep the sheep – and the public – out.

But it was immediately after the First World War that the great invasion took place. The war had revealed a desperate need for home-grown timber. The Forestry Commission was set up, and before the end of 1933 they had planted more than five million spruce and nearly one and a quarter million larches in two areas, on either side of Bassenthwaite Lake and at the head of Ennerdale Valley.

There was little initial protest, but in 1935 when it became known that the Forestry Commission had bought 7,000 acres of Eskdale and Dunnerdale and planned to plant extensively there, a tidal wave of opposition began to gather. Its leading spokesman and moving spirit was a remarkable man, the Reverend H. H. Symonds.

Symonds had been a distinguished scholar and teacher. He took a First in Greats at Oxford, taught the Classical Sixth at Rugby, and became headmaster of schools at Chester and Liverpool. At the age of 50 he retired to live at Wood Close above Grasmere and make a full-time occupation of what he called 'rescuing scraps of natural beauty'. He had an aesthetic appreciation of the Lakeland landscape and a deep regard for the hill shepherds, the 'masters of Herdwicks', and their ancient way of life. In 1933 he published *Walking in the Lake District* which is still arguably the best, and certainly the best-written walkers' guidebook – witty and clear-eyed and outspoken, massively authoritative, crammed with information and opinion, enlivened by wide-ranging references, Classical and Biblical and other. His love for the District shines through but it is never sentimental or blinkered. In an appendix he discussed the idea of making the Lake District a national park:

> The case for the protection of the Lake District as a national park ... is an extraordinarily strong one .... But the only hope is in the driving force of a well informed and well organised public opinion. For though the problem is complex and difficult, and the general principles can only be applied by experts and through technical knowledge, yet the main thing which we all want is clear: hence the importance of some thoroughly national group of Friends of the Lake District, to supply the emotional impetus without which skill and knowledge win no victories.

Within a year of publication the Friends of the Lake District was formed. There had been predecessors of a kind – a Lake District Defence Society in the 1880s, the Lake District Safeguarding Society launched by Canon Rawnsley after the First World War. But the Friends were different – bigger, more tightly organised, altogether more formidable. Symonds helped draft their constitution. He was their first Treasurer, then their Secretary. For 25 years, until his death in 1958, he was their protagonist, a tireless and fearless campaigner.

Very quickly the Friends found themselves with a major battle on their hands, against the Forestry Commission's plans for Eskdale and Dunnerdale. They got in touch with other objectors, the Herdwick Sheep Breeders' Association and the Council for the Protection of Rural England, and a joint committee was set up. They offered the Forestry Commission a compromise and it was rejected. Then they organised a petition and secured 13,000 signatures. This was presented in October 1935 but had no effect. In August 1936 the Commission published a White Paper, outlining its plans and making it clear they had no intention of making any real concessions. This inspired Symonds to a period of intense writing. Before the year's end his thundering and magisterial reply was published, *Afforestation in the Lake District*.

He opened with a resounding declaration of modern man's need for the wilderness:

> As man civilises, his desire for wild and primitive beauty becomes greater: we guard ourselves in this way against insanity, and remain what we must in part always be, earth-born. If we forget our origins, it is at a great cost. Those instincts which crowd us together and socialize us satisfy a part only of our inherited needs: isolation, awe, and adventure, and to feel the unaltered, age-long beauty of the external world, are no less a part of sound and satisfying life. All places of retreat and freedom, where we are not reminded of the man-made world, become of greater value to us as assimilation, crowding and routine increase.

He spoke of the smallness of the Lake District, its beauty and its vulnerability. Part of the beauty, he said, sprang from the deciduous trees in all their variety and splendour. This could not be said of the conifer forests:

> The planting is continuous, by the square mile. Where there was colour, this is first hidden, then dissolved: grasses, moss, plant-life perish as the trees form a canopy. Rock and scree, blue, grey, or violet, are still there, but hidden. What is seen is the rigid and monotonous ranks of spruce, dark green to blackish, goose-stepping on the fell side. Their colour – you must except the larch – is in effect one steady tone all round the dull year: there are no glories of spring and autumn for the conifer. Sunlight, which a broadleafed, deciduous tree reflects and vivifies, is annihilated on their absorbent texture: on a bright landscape they are so much blotting paper. Bird life perishes, for there

are no berried trees, as plant life perishes: the barren undergrowth of a coniferous woodland is a pale, bloodless thing. And to the long unbroken mileage of drab, dead colour, with the sitka spruce king of this gloomy kingdom, you must add the curse of uniformity in growth. For conifers are patterned trees, branching evenly and subservient to arboreal geometry. The beech, you may say, makes rules of growth only to break them; but these conifers are of a type, perfectly well behaved and bad company.

Further on, he describes Ennerdale as it must have looked to Coleridge when he surveyed the valley from the foot of the lake, before the Forestry Commission transformed it:

From the summit of the Pillar range the fells drop without a pause to the valley bottom. Trigonometry gives the net rise as a mere 2,200 feet, but the canons of beauty are negligent of this arithmetic: in Nature's architecture, which has another scale, the Pillar range stands up in stupendous command. And the grandeur is an effect of contrasts of bare slope in the lower contours and a serrated skyline of the volcanic rock above: in between is steep, broken crag, set among the colours of the fell side: here and there a vertical stream bed, or a fan of scree spilled into the grass and bracken of the lower, horizontal slopes, pulls the wide extension of the valley bottom into unity with the crag and steepness far above: there is great composition.

Symonds hated the conifer incursion for many reasons – because the trees themselves were ugly and dull and uniform; because their straight lines, in the planting and in the forest boundaries, were unnatural; because they either destroyed, or at best discouraged other forms of life, both plant and animal; because they dispossessed the Herdwick sheep and their shepherds.

He hated them, too, because they denied large areas of fellside to the walker. One of the great traditional virtues of the

Lake District is the fact that the hills are open and free to all. Once he is above the valley bottom and beyond the 'in-take wall', which marks the frontier of the fields around the farm where hay is grown and the ewes are grazed at lambing time, the walker can go where he wants. He may be asked or advised to use the established paths, but there is no compulsion to do so and in many places there are no paths anyway. 'Every man his own path-maker,' as Coleridge quoted.

In other parts of Britain – in the Peak District, for example, and in Scotland – there have been fierce territorial battles between determined ramblers and land-owners insistent on the rights of privacy and the laws of trespass. There has been next to nothing of this in the Lake District story. But this time-honoured freedom of the fells was lost wherever the Forestry Commission moved in. Their plantations were fenced to protect young trees from the predatory sheep. They laid their forest tracks in brutally straight lines. If you try to leave the track, you soon find the going impossibly hard. Symonds found it intolerable:

> Like all others who love and know the district, I abominate this regimentation and cross-gartering of tracks, and hanker for the old-fashioned, skimble-skamble, bandy-legged divergences which took us as the spirit moved or the slope invited . . .

He used yet another telling argument. He was not, he said, against conifer forests as such. They were clearly needed. They might even be aesthetically acceptable in Scandinavia or the European Alps or in the great spaces of the Scottish Highlands and Lowlands. But in the Lake District, where the summits were comparatively low and distances comparatively small, conifer forests of the size the Commission planted were grotesquely out of proportion to the landscape.

He built a powerful case and he argued it with great force. It won the day – not a total victory but a considerable one. The Forestry Commission promised that it would not seek to acquire land in the central 300 square miles of the District, an area which contains the high mountains and the valleys of Ullswater,

Borrowdale, Buttermere, Wastwater and Langdale. As far as the land they had already bought in Eskdale and Dunnerdale was concerned, they promised to consult with the Council for the Protection of Rural England about the areas to be planted and the species of tree to be used.

In the event, there was only limited planting in Eskdale and the vital area, the magnificent valley head, was spared completely. There was more planting in Dunnerdale, the Duddon Valley, but the promised consultations did take place and the job was done more sensitively than it had been done in Ennerdale.

The great battle of the mid-1930s was not the end of the conifer conflict. In lesser ways it still goes on. But the Commission seem to have learned the fundamental lesson that in the Lake District they will not be allowed to buy whatever land they want and plant however they wish. They tread more carefully now. They run Visitors' Centres to explain their work and win public sympathy. They intermix broadleaf trees with their conifers, a minimum of 5 per cent, they claim, and up to 20 per cent in some places. They make more effort to plant along the contours rather than in regimental straight lines. They also, they say, mix trees of different ages together to lend some variety to the scene. These policies sometimes seem more apparent on the pages of their brochures than on the fellsides. But the effort is undoubtedly being made. They are kept on their toes by the knowledge that everything they do in the Lake District is scrutinised by Mrs Susan Johnson, the daughter of Reverend H. H. Symonds, in whom the spirit of her father goes marching vigilantly on.

CHAPTER FIVE

To the Coast

$\mathbf{O}$n the second day of his walk Coleridge once again delayed his departure until the afternoon. He spent the morning with John Ponsonby, looking at the lake and the mountains and listening to the old man's stories. Now, still heading westwards, he left the high ground behind him and made for the coast:

> I left Long Moor after Tea, and proceeded to Egremont, 5 miles – thro' a very pleasant Country, part of the way by the River Enna [Ehen], with well wooded Banks, and nice green Fields, and pretty Houses with Trees, and two huge Sail-cloth Manufactories . . .

For the next two days his route lay outside the Lake District. The country there was, and still is, very different – richer, greener farmland and more populous towns and villages along the industrialised coastal strip. Coleridge's comments, in his *Notebook* and in his letter to Sara, are fewer and briefer. It was the least stimulating part of his walk.

Even so, it was undoubtedly pleasanter going in 1802 than it is today. He advanced along grassy tracks and quiet country lanes, with occasional farms and villages to enliven the scene. Today, except for very short stretches, you have no alternative but to walk on the hard, metalled road. There are no pavements or grass verges, and the traffic is almost continuous.

At first, leaving Ennerdale Bridge, I tried to follow the riverside path. There were encouraging signs saying 'Pedestrians', but the route they indicated led me across a couple of fields to a muddy ditch with a new wire fence beyond. I had to negotiate the ditch and climb over the fence to gain the river bank. Here I found a lone angler, practising disappointment with the patience of his kind. He told me the river held salmon, trout and sea trout, but he had no evidence. He said there was a path of sorts along the river but it was a rough one, not to be recommended if you were carrying a fishing rod. It was not to be recommended if you were carrying a loaded rucksack either. The ground rose and dipped steeply. The slopes were slimy and the level stretches boggy. Frequent patches of nettles made me glad I was not wearing shorts. A cloud of insects swarmed persistently around as I sweated and clawed my way through a tangled undergrowth of brambles and wild roses.

I had walked this way a few years before and it had been a pleasant and easily managed path – much the same, I imagine, as it was for Coleridge. Since then, though, there had been much so-called development, the laying of pipes and cables, and the churning about of bulldozers, resulting in that particularly obnoxious kind of devastation you often get when the rural and the urban collide. The old path was virtually destroyed. I stuck to it, as best I could, for half a mile or so, and then decided to climb a stone wall, cross a field, and clamber over another wall to gain the road. I saw no sign of Coleridge's 'huge Sail-cloth Manufactories' which must have supplied the ship-building industry around Whitehaven.

The road follows the line of the river, sometimes right alongside, sometimes 100 yards or so above it. I passed notices saying 'Caravan Club. Members Only' and 'Ennerdale Anglers' Association. No canoeing'. The grass was much lusher here than it is in the higher valleys, and there was a variety of livestock: Friesian and shaggy Highland cattle and many of those sturdy, off-white beasts who testify to the recent popularity of the Charolais strain; two doleful donkeys in a field; poultry of all kinds, ranging freely; four plump turkeys, one of them making a very nasty noise. There was not a rambler to be seen.

I leant against a wall to make notes, and two girls came down the field and climbed the stile to the road. Each had a plastic bag full of field mushrooms; it was a wonderful season for mushrooms, as it seemed to be for everything else. I asked about the harvest but they were more interested in me:

'Where are you from?'

'Keswick. I walked from there to Ennerdale Bridge yesterday.'

'In all that weather?'

'Yes. I got rather wet.'

'Aa would say. Are you sleeping rough?'

'I didn't last night – it was too wet. But if the weather brightens up I probably will in the next few days.'

They wanted to know about my journey and, when I told them, clearly thought it was daft. They had never heard of Coleridge.

They jumped on their bicycles and pedalled off towards Egremont.

Further on I paused to admire the lovely, double-arched sandstone bridge that spans the river below Cleator Moor. Beyond it, long, low terraced rows of workers' cottages spread themselves across the hillside. This is where, approaching from the east, industrial West Cumbria first shows itself. Until the first decades of this century Cleator Moor was a busy little town with blast furnaces and mines for coal and iron ore. The place is celebrated in one of Norman Nicholson's early poems:

> From one shaft at Cleator Moor
> They mined for coal and iron ore.
> This harvest below ground could show
> Black and red currants on one tree.
>
> In furnaces they burnt the coal,
> The ore was smelted into steel,
> And railway lines from end to end
> Corseted the bulging land ...

This land was rich in minerals and the exploitation continued well into the twentieth century: the remains are still visible in pit-heads and heaps of spoil and derelict factories. Norman Nicholson spent all his life in the iron ore town of Millom, further down the coast. He was born in 1914 in a terraced house in the town centre, and he died in the same house in 1987. No one observed the industrial coastland more keenly than he did and no one wrote about it, in prose as well as poetry, more powerfully. He travelled inland as well, ranging across Cumberland and Westmorland, studying the geology and the lie of the land, steeping himself in its history, listening to the chat of the working folk. His distinctive voice – quiet and throaty and strong – is inescapable in many places as you travel around Cumbria today.

It is arguable, probable even, that we should have had little or none of this writing had it not been for the fact that he was struck down, at the age of 16, by tuberculosis. He was doing well at school and destined for university, and it seems almost certain that he would have gone on to become a teacher. Instead, he spent nearly two years in a sanatorium in the New Forest, his only extended absence from Cumberland. The sickness left him so frail that it was impossible for him to contemplate a regular, full-time job. Gradually he took to writing. His first collection of poems was published in 1944. It was called *Five Rivers* and the title poem, by a happy chance, describes the rivers that flow into the Irish Sea in this region, rivers that Coleridge crossed in his 'circumcursion':

Southwards from Whitehaven, where cliffs of coal
Slant like shale to the low black mole,
The railway canters along the curving shore
Over five rivers, which slowly pour
On the steps of the shingle where the grey gulls bask:
EHEN and CALDER, IRT and MITE and ESK ...

Passing Cleator Moor, I saw children paddling and splashing each other in the shallows of the Ehen. An elderly man was sitting on a bench, watching the children and enjoying the sunshine. I had no doubt which was the right way but wanted to speak to someone:

'Is this the road to Egremont?'

'Keep straight on,' he said firmly. 'You can't go nowhere else.'

An hour later I was mounting the steep hill that leads to the centre of the ancient market town. But Coleridge did not stop at Egremont this time, so neither did I. Pausing only to buy an ice-cream cornet, I marched along the wide, handsome main street, then turned right to find the road to St Bees.

It is only 4 miles or so, through farmland with grazing cattle and fields of corn and potato. For a while the prospect ahead was dominated by a line of tall pylons, striding northwards in pairs. It is a sight that never fails to bring to mind the odd but haunting metaphor that Stephen Spender used in the 1930s:

Pylons, those pillars
Bare like nude, giant girls that have no secret.

The image seems entirely inappropriate to me now. Pylons do not look anything like big naked girls. But, though it must be nearly half a century since I first read those lines, I have never forgotten them. I suppose they had such an impact on me because I was 14 or so at the time and had been brought up in a home of strict Methodist propriety and prudery. Nude girls played no active part in my life – except in my mind where they were very active indeed – so it was exciting just to see the words in print.

A mile further on, the nuclear processing complex at Sellafield came into view to the south; the smooth-backed hump of Black Combe – Norman Nicholson's neighbour mountain – behind it. For the next three days of the walk it would be impossible to forget Sellafield for long. All along the coast, and even from the slopes and summits of the high fells of the Lake District, it is obtrusively in view, its cooling towers ceaselessly emitting their clouds of steam. Though the road I was walking was little more than a country lane, it was alive with fast-moving cars, all heading my way – day-shift workers from Sellafield hurrying home to tea.

I was near the coast now and the breeze was stronger. Soon I could see the sparkling, silvery waters of the Irish Sea. But the hills of the Isle of Man, a few miles due west, were invisible. The sky in that direction was black with clouds. Another dose of Atlantic weather was on the way.

The final part of the road skirts along the cliff top. To the left I could look down on white breakers continually pounding the shore. Ahead lay the sweep of St Bees bay and, beyond that, the steep, red, sandstone cliffs of the headland. Two lads nearby were flying a bright yellow, long-tailed kite, very successfully. There was no one on the beach.

Just as the road begins to dip down to the town you pass a row of modern bungalows. Such building would be prohibited in the Lake District as alien and out of character, but I was outside the boundaries of the National Park now. Some of the names on the bungalows suggested that their owners rather wished they had been able to afford to build in hotter, more exotic places – 'Canzone del Mare', for example, and 'Miramare'.

It was beginning to drizzle in a half-hearted way as I descended into St Bees, which has a rather bleak and windswept air at the best of times. The first two bed and breakfast places I tried were already full – one of them of Sellafield workers, lodging there on a semi-permanent basis – and I began to fear a repetition of the previous evening's struggles. But then I was directed to Stone House Farm, an early eighteenth-century building which – although it stands in the middle of the town – still operates as a farm, mainly sheep and horses.

I was shown to the spacious ground-floor front room which had all I needed to make tea and coffee and, of course, a television set. I watched the evening news bulletin. One of the great differences, it occurred to me, between Coleridge's journey and mine was that he was easily able to get away from his normal life in a way that would hardly be possible today. For the nine days of his absence he had no news of family or friends and probably heard nothing of what was happening to the country or the world at large. In contrast, I kept in continuous, almost immediate touch with national and international affairs by television or radio or newspapers, and the telephone made it easy to get all the family and local news. I was grateful for the latter facility, but could well have done without the former. The week's news was of continued internecine strife in the Lebanon and in Northern Ireland; revelations of police malpractice in the West Midlands; the execution of more young dissidents in China; British ports refusing entry to a cargo of toxic waste from Canada; England's cricketers concluding a disastrous season by losing the final Test against Australia by an innings and 180 runs.

I had a long, hot bath, soaking the aches away, and reflecting that here was another important contrast. Hot baths had become a matter of increasing importance to me as the years passed. However fit I may be, a day's hard walking is sure to stiffen up the muscles, and if I stop for a rest en route, there are always a few creaky moments before the legs get going again. Without a bath in the evening, there is a danger of cramps in the night and the certainty that getting going again next morning will entail several minutes of mild muscular pain. Coleridge, however, makes no mention, on this walk or any of the others, of ever having a bath or even a hot-water wash. Hot water was harder to come by in those days, and people were less concerned with personal hygiene than we are now. More than two decades after the 'circumcursion', the venerable Dr Martin Routh, President of Magdalen College, Oxford, from 1791 to 1854, refused to provide baths in the college on the grounds that the young men were only there for two months at a time.

His visit to St Bees was the low point of Coleridge's journey. The accommodation he found was abysmal and expensive. He told Sara Hutchinson:

> ... the whole of my expences at St. Bees, a glass of Gin and Water, my Bed, and Breakfast amounted to 11d ... when I came there could not get a Bed – at last got an apology for one, at a miserable Pot-house; slept, or rather dozed in my Clothes – breakfasted there – and went to the School and Church ruins – had read in the history of Cumbd; that there was an 'excellent Library presented to the School by Sr. James Lowther', which proved to be some 30 odd Volumes of commentaries on the Scripture utterly worthless – and which with all my passion for ragged old Folios I should certainly make serviceable ... for fire-lighting.

The three dots before the concluding words mark the place where he inked out two or three words. It looks as though he were suggesting some more fundamental use for the 'ragged old

Folios' when he thought better of it and revised his wording. The books remained on the shelves of the school library, rarely consulted, until a few years ago when they were transferred for safer keeping to Newcastle University. Sir James Lowther, who is mentioned in Hutchinson's *History of Cumberland* as having presented the books to the school, was the first Earl of Lonsdale, by far the richest and most powerful man in Cumberland. He was also the most awful, a prime example of the privileged lout. Contemporaries knew him as 'Wicked Jimmy', the 'Bad Earl' and the 'Tyrant of the North'. His great wealth, deriving from the vast estates and rich coastal collieries he had inherited, did nothing to restrain his greed and ruthlessness. His political power – he had total control over nine seats in the House of Commons – gained him his earldom. It was he who had employed the Wordsworths' father as political agent in Cockermouth and who, when John Wordsworth died in 1783, refused to hand over to the family the large sum, £5,000, that he owed. There was a ferocious legal battle, but it was not until after the Earl's death in May 1802 that the Wordsworth children finally got the money they were owed, plus interest.

Coleridge's *Notebook* makes no mention of his stay at St Bees. There is only one short entry for this period and it is so cryptic as to be, to me at least, quite impenetrable:

> Motion of objects present and not present, in a half drunken mood, when we would be glad to go to sleep, represents, in the clouds, rapid motion simply presence, and the feeling of the absence and the presence –

'Suck any sense from that who can.' I certainly cannot. It seems possible that there is something awry with the punctuation; perhaps the comma after 'clouds' should have been an apostrophe, and there should be a comma after the word 'motion'. It would make the sentence a little more grammatical but hardly more intelligible. The likeliest explanation, to my prosaic mind, is that Coleridge drank rather too much, in his efforts to get to sleep that night, and then, half awake, tried to jot down some abstruse idea that had come to him. All too often, in my experience, the 'great thoughts' that come to one in the night are shown to be either trite or meaningless when you read them in the cold light of the morning after.

Unlike Coleridge I slept comfortably and soundly, ate a large breakfast and then went out to look round.

St Bees is set back from the sea, an odd, straggly, unfocused sort of place, but it has a long history and some impressive buildings and ruins to prove it.

A woman missionary from Ireland, St Bega, is said to have founded a nunnery here in the mid-seventh century and given her name to the town. In the twelfth century William de Meschines returned from crusading to build himself a castle in Egremont and a priory at St Bees, both in the distinctive red sandstone of the area. When the monasteries were dissolved by Henry VIII the priory fell into elegant ruins. The priory church, though, became the parish church of St Mary and St Bega, which it remains to this day. It contains some Norman windows and a superb west doorway, elaborately designed and intricately carved. W. G. Collingwood, in *The Lake Counties*, said it was 'a very fine relic of the Middle Ages'. Nikolaus Pevsner, who was not easily moved to enthusiasm, described the doorway as 'the richest in the county' (the Cumberland and Westmorland volume of his *Buildings of England* series, 1967). This whole area, the church and the adjoining ruins, has a powerful atmosphere of antiquity and serenity. But Coleridge was unimpressed. He was intent on the old folio books and took no interest at all in ancient buildings, unless there was some story or mystery attached to them which might excite his imagination.

St Bees School is close by and it was here that Coleridge went to be disappointed by the 'utterly worthless' old volumes. The school was founded by Edmund Grindal, said (by some) to have been born in Finkle Street, St Bees, in 1517. He became a priest and managed to survive the manifold religious dangers of those days to become Archbishop of Canterbury in 1575. Eight years after his enthronement, remembering his county of origin, he established a grammar school at St Bees, offering free education to boys from Cumberland and Westmorland. Part of the school's original Foundation House remains and the whole presents a handsome frontage, with castellated turrets and a tower, all in red sandstone. Education is far from being free here nowadays. It is a public school, taking girls as well as boys; boarders and day pupils. Its most famous old boy of modern times is the comic actor Rowan Atkinson, widely known (and not easily forgotten) for his portrayal of Blackadder on television.

It is at the coast, a quarter of a mile from the school, that St Bees is seen at its most desolate. It must have been spectacular at one time, a wide sweeping bay with cliffs at either side, but it has been sadly brutalised by a monstrous concrete sea wall with a large car park behind it. A hotel and a row of lodging houses face the sea and the prevailing wind. I saw only two people on the front, middle-aged men unloading their rucksacks from the boot of a car and setting off up the headland path, the first steps of the coast-to-coast walk.

After his terrible night in the 'miserable Pot-house', Coleridge was in no mood to be impressed by anything. In his letter to Sara he expressed his anger with William Hutchinson, whose words had sent him off on the long detour to find the old folios:

> Men who write tours and County histories I have by woeful experience found out to be *damned Liars*, harsh words, but true! – It was a wet woeful oppressive morning – I was sore with my bad night – walked down to the Beach, which is a very nice hard Sand for more than a mile, but the St. Bees Head which I had read much of as a noble Cliff, might be made a song of on the Flats of the Dutch Coast – but in England 'twill scarcely bear a looking-at.

The walk back to Egremont takes just over an hour and this, too, Coleridge found 'miserable'. He decided to go no further that day, the third day of the walk. He ate dinner, then went to look at the ruins of the castle. There he sat down with his *Notebook*:

> View, from Egremont Castle, of Houses and River and

Hill. Fields beyond River, as impossible to describe to an other as a Dream ...

He attempted a description just the same:

The fine noble Ash Tree in the Road between the Castle Hill and the Buildings – the Buildings, Wall, Garden with its various beds – so slovenly in its tyr-annically straight parallelogram inclosures, the Mary-golds, yellow Lillies, loftiest Peas in Blossom, Beans, Onions, Cabbages – then the Houses – in such various outlines, all formal, yet the formality neutralized by the variety of the formal and their incursions on each other – some thatched, some slated, some meeting the eye with their broad fronts, some with their corner Gavels – some spank new, some in ruins .... here the Hills and fields peeping over the Town, here the higher houses intercepting the Hills and Fields. The country itself banks above banks in harmonious Irregularity.

To Sara he wrote:

... visited the Castle, the Views from which are uncommonly interesting – I looked thro' an old wild Arch – slovenly black Houses, and gardens, as wild as a Dream, over the hills beyond them ...

I cheated a little at this point in the journey. Coleridge spent his third night in Egremont recovering from the previous night. But the distance from St Bees is under 4 miles and, although I made a detour – along the cliffs for a mile or so, then inland through ancient sunken tracks between high hedgerows – I reached Egremont by 11 a.m. I knew that for the next few miles, heading south, it would be impossible to get off the busy main coastal road. I also knew that the weather forecast for the next day was bad. And I was aware that Coleridge's fourth day was a longer one, down the coast for some 5 miles, then a further 7 miles inland to the head of the Wasdale Valley. I felt fit and vigorous and the sun was shining fitfully so I pushed on to Calder Bridge.

It was unpleasant going. The coast road, the A595, is not wide but it carries a heavy burden of traffic, much of it lorries serving Sellafield. They travel fast and the blast of their slip-stream hits you in the back like an over-hearty friend. They spread dust and din and the smells of internal combustion. Coleridge, in contrast, found the walk from Egremont 'pleasant' and told Sara in his letter:

> Indeed the whole way from Egremont I had beautiful
> Sea Views, the low hills to my right dipping down into
> inverted Arches, or Angles, and the Sea, often with a
> Ship seen thro' – while on my left the Steeple, and
> Sca'Fell facing each other far above the other Fells,
> formed in their interspace a great Gap in the Heaven.

For the most part the passing traffic prevented my seeing the sea at all, but when I did there was never a ship in sight. To my left the high fells of Lakeland were clearly visible. As I advanced, the view ahead was increasingly dominated by the towers and domes and buildings of Sellafield, which lies between the village of Calder Bridge and the coast.

The nuclear processing plant at Sellafield is Cumbria's most divisive and controversial issue. It began, after the Second World War, as a factory to produce plutonium for Britain's atomic armoury. In the 1950s it became a power plant, using atomic fission to provide energy for the National Grid, and its birth was attended by a wave of euphoria: the magical new source of power would, it was widely believed, prove cleaner and cheaper and safer than its predecessors, coal and oil; we were no longer totally dependent on the fossil fuels which were bound to be expended in the next century; Britain was leading the world in the new technology. Now, they say, it supplies one-fifth of Britain's power. In the 1980s another role has been added – reprocessing spent nuclear fuel and disposing of the poisonous waste. In this department, it is claimed, contracts have already been signed – with Japan and Germany and other countries – that will earn £5 billion in the next ten years. Sellafield gives employment to 14,000 people, in a region that would have been in great distress without it. It has brought many highly educated and intelligent scientists to the area. It has given generously to deserving local causes. It has a Visitors Centre which attracted 160,000 people in 1989.

But there is, as everybody knows, another side to the argument. There was a very serious fire in 1957 and a leakage of radioactivity that affected the region for many miles around. The authorities tried to hush it all up and then to minimise it. There have been further though lesser leaks since. Poisonous waste was pumped out into the Irish Sea so no one wanted to buy its fish and many were reluctant to swim there. British Nuclear Fuels claim that radioactive emissions into the atmosphere are too small to worry about, but their opponents produce figures to show that the incidence of cancer among Sellafield workers is higher than the national average and the incidence of leukaemia among children growing up in the region is considerably higher. Some of the waste from reprocessing will have to be securely stored for a million years, and it is not particularly reassuring to be told that they have been successfully storing waste for 30 years already.

The debate is bedevilled by several factors. Most of us cannot begin to understand the processes of nuclear reaction and their possible consequences, and we are wary of the unknown. Many associate atomic fission with the bombs that destroyed Hiroshima and Nagasaki in 1945. There is a healthy, and justified, reluctance to believe the authorities when they make soothing noises. Why would they spend £5 million on a Visitors Centre if they have nothing to hide? And why do they keep changing the name of the place? First it was Calder Hall, then Windscale, now Sellafield. Sometimes they give the impression of being more concerned with cleaning up their image than cleaning up their act.

It is strange to reflect that the man who started it all, the father of the atomic theory, was a Cumbrian in origin and a contemporary of Coleridge's. John Dalton was born in 1766 at Eaglesfield, a village near Cockermouth. He was a mathematician and scientist. In 1803 he went to lecture at the Royal Institution in London where he became a friend and colleague of Coleridge's friend, Humphry Davy. Five years later he produced his theory of the indivisible atom as the basic building block of all matter, which he had developed as a way of explaining the facts of chemical combination.

It is impossible to be sure what line Coleridge would have taken in the great debate over nuclear power. He would certainly have been fascinated by atomic science, and most likely would have drawn abstruse metaphysical conclusions from it about the nature of reality and God. He was a natural adventurer, intellectually as well as physically, and I am inclined to think that he would have been in favour of continuing with the efforts to produce power from nuclear processes. After all, what progress could humankind have made if the man who first discovered fire had suppressed his findings on the grounds that it was dangerous and destructive?

There is no doubt what Norman Nicholson thought about nuclear power. In his book *Greater Lakeland*, published in 1969, he wrote:

> In spite of all the new money and the new faces, Calder Hall darkens the landscape like a threat. It is not that the buildings themselves are ugly, except for the clutter of car parks and dumps and wire-netting at the periphery. The original towers – now, apparently, already out of date – were slim and elegant, and the new cooling towers, though less pleasing in shape, often turn the coast into a Chinese watercolour with their twisting wraiths of mist. But when there was an atomic leak at the plant in the late fifties, and we, in Millom, had to pour our milk down the drains, we felt as if we were waiting for lightning to strike from a clear sky. There was no recognisable sign of danger, but the air seemed electric. The atom, in fact, is not a comfortable neighbour.

Back Into the Hills

Coleridge had a good night's sleep in Egremont and set off on the fourth day of his walk greatly refreshed:

> ... had a good Bed, slept well – and left Egremont this morning after Breakfast, had a pleasant walk to Calder Abbey – an elegant but not very interesting Ruin, joining to a very hansome Gentleman's House built of red free-stone, which has the comfortable warm look of Brick without its meanness and multitude of puny squares....

Clearly, he was more impressed by the newly built mansion than he was by what was left of the ancient abbey. He had never been carried away by the eighteenth-century passion for medieval ruins. Wealthy land-owners had them specially built on their estates to give the place 'atmosphere' and 'quaintness'. Novelists of the 'Gothick horror' school – gently mocked by Jane Austen in *Northanger Abbey* – thrilled countless readers with their strange tales in such settings.

William Hutchinson, in his *History of Cumberland*, entered fully into the spirit of the age and the place:

> ... In this parish are the remains of CALDER ABBEY, distant from the road about a mile, and situated on the northern banks of the river Calder, in a narrow valley, inclosed with fine hanging woods, but in marshy and ill-chosen ground. The seclusion of the place, and still and solemn retirement, were well adapted to the austerities and religious rules of the monks of the Cistercian order, who were placed here ....
>
> In this situation, the solemn ruins seemed to stand mourning in their sacred solitude, concealing woe in the secluded valley, and bending to the adversity of

— 114 —

ages; like the image of Melancholy, looking down desponding, on the tomb of interred honours and wasted ornaments.

Hutchinson goes on to give a detailed description of the ruins which makes it clear that they have been considerably diminished in the past two centuries, presumably by people wanting the stones for building. They are still beautiful, though, and highly evocative, recalling the line from Shakespeare's sonnet: 'Bare ruined choirs where late the sweet birds sang.'

The walk there from the village is beautiful too, along the northern bank of the river by a gravel path in the shade of mature trees. The river is strong and lively, with many deep pools and glistening mossy rocks.

The Cistercians built close to rivers. Calder Abbey, founded in the twelfth century, stands in open meadowland with a circle of broadleaf trees beyond. They built in the local sandstone and solidly, but today the walls and arches and colonnades are open to the sky and the elements. Ferns and grasses grow along the tops of the walls, and the weathering of the centuries has turned the stone grey in many places.

The house, which butts right up against the abbey wall, is a much brighter red. It was built in 1770 or thereabouts for Mr J. T. Senhouse, a member of one of West Cumberland's leading families. It is an imposing Georgian pile, and the massive central porch has Tuscan columns supporting a Classical pediment. When I passed by, the place had a run-down, dilapidated air. Sheep grazed the long grass where the front lawns used to be. All approach gates were firmly padlocked and the main entrance had a notice saying 'Private residence'. Local folk know little about the house now. It was sold, they say, towards the end of the 1960s, but the owners rarely visit and the building is looked after by a caretaker and his family who keep themselves very much to themselves.

Coleridge looked round the area, noting in particular an 'interesting Mill' which is now a garage, and Ponsonby Hall, which has been acquired by British Nuclear Fuels. Ponsonby is one of the recurring names in this region – they were the great land-owners in the time of King Stephen and Henry I. Towards the end of the fourteenth century the manor was bought by Nicholas Stanley, who founded a very durable dynasty. Hutchinson gives pages of family detail and concludes:

> By this genealogical account, it appears that there have been 23 generations in 756 years, and that the property of this part of the family, who fixed in Cumberland, has descended regularly from father to son to the present possessor ... for 449 years.

There are still farmers in the area by the name of Stanley, and I spent the night at the Stanley Arms Hotel, which stands between the river and the main road. The ancestral home of this branch of the family, Dalegarth Hall in Eskdale, is still occupied by Stanleys.

Coleridge pushed on southwards:

> I regained the Road, and came to Bonewood, a single Alehouse on the top of the hill above the Village Gosforth – drank a pint of Beer [...] – from this Bonewood is a noble view of the Isle of Man on the one side, and on the other all the bold dread tops of the Ennerdale and Wastdale Mountains.

That was in his letter. In the *Notebook* he said he arrived at the pub – 'a neat little public House kept by one Manson' – at 11 a.m. on Wednesday. He fell into conversation with a woman:

> Lost her son, last new year's day 7 year, in Bassenthwaite, attempting to save Dr. Head of Cockermouth and another Gentleman [from drowning] – they saved, and he lost – consoled the old Mother by contrasting his Fate with a Soldier's dying in attempting to kill his fellow creatures.

He dropped down to Gosforth, then turned eastwards, heading for Wasdale Head at the very heart of the high fells:

> ... the huge enormous mountains of Wast dale all bare and iron-red – and on them a *forest* of cloud-

shadows, all motionless – a low Ridge intercepts the Lake from the eye – to my right and to my left rough stony Common with great Knots, raggedly cloathed with underwood ... Mem. beautiful shadow of the Fern upon the lichened Stone which it overcanopied. The Seaward view very nicely wooded – 3 Ships in view – 4 one horse carts in a file on the top of the Fell to my Left, 3 boys, each one on his Horse, one Girl in her cart – picturesque.

You can sense Coleridge's spirits rising as he made for the mountains. He was getting into his stride by now, and so was I. One of the special delights of distance walking is that after a while the legs take over the labour of locomotion, allowing the mind to roam at will. On level ground you can put your legs into automatic and let them get on with it. On steeper, rougher ground you have to be careful where you are placing your feet, but one small corner of the brain will attend to that while the rest of it ponders and muses, observes and considers, reflects and reminisces. Walking is, after all, our most natural form of exercise. The solitary walker, beholden to no one, can strike his own rhythm and set his own pace. He fills his lungs with fresh air and feasts his eyes on the passing scene. It induces a kind of mental activity, lively but serene, that cannot easily be engendered in any other way. Many walker/writers have found it so.

Seventy years before Coleridge made his long walk, Jean-Jacques Rousseau, the prophet and precursor of the Romantic Movement, was walking vigorously and alone about the foothills of the Alps and across France. He later wrote:

Never did I think so much, exist so vividly, and experience so much, never have I been so much myself – if I may use that expression – as in the journeys I have taken alone and on foot. There is something about walking which stimulates and enlivens my thoughts. When I stay in one place I can hardly think at all; my body has to be on the move to set my mind going. The sight of the countryside, the succession of pleasant views, the open air, a sound appetite, and the good health I gain by walking, the easy atmosphere of an inn, the absence of everything that makes me feel my dependence, of everything that recalls me to my situation – all these serve to free my spirit, to lend a greater boldness to my thinking, to throw me, so to speak, into the vastness of things, so that I can combine them, select them, and make them mine as I will, without fear or restraint.

It could be Coleridge himself speaking, the Coleridge who wrote in a letter to Thomas Wedgwood, dated 14th January 1803:

In simple earnest, I never find myself alone within the embracement of rocks and hills, a traveller up an alpine road, but my spirit courses, drives and eddies, like a Leaf in Autumn: a wild activity, of thoughts, imaginations, feelings, and impulses of motion, rises up from within me – a sort of *bottom-wind* that blows to no point of the compass, and comes from I know not whence, but agitates the whole of me; my whole Being is filled with waves.... The farther I ascend from animated Nature, from men, and cattle, and the common birds of the woods and fields, the greater becomes in me the Intensity of the feeling of Life....

Thomas De Quincey, who was a considerable pedestrian himself, says that Coleridge's style of walking made him an awkward companion. Apparently he tended to veer from side to side with little regard for those he was with, 'meandering with a mazy motion' like the river he describes in 'Kubla Khan'. In his *Recollections of the Lake Poets*, De Quincey also gives a lively account of Wordsworth's appearance and the therapeutic benefits he derived from daily walks:

His legs were pointedly condemned by all the female connoisseurs in legs that ever I heard lecture upon that topic; not that they were bad in any way that would force itself upon your notice – there was no absolute deformity about them; and undoubtedly they had been serviceable legs beyond the average standard of human requisition; for I calculate, upon good data, that with these identical legs Wordsworth must have traversed a distance of 175 to 180,000 English miles – a mode of exertion which, to him, stood in the stead of wine, spirits and all other stimulants whatsoever to the animal spirits; to which he has been indebted for a life of unclouded happiness, and we for much of what is most excellent in his writings.

De Quincey was an accomplished and amusing writer, always happy to exaggerate if he felt it would enliven the reader's interest. It is not easy to believe that Wordsworth, at the age of 70 or thereabouts, had covered 180,000 miles on foot. It would imply that from the age of ten onwards he averaged some 8 miles a day.

There is much to be said, and much has been said, in praise of hill-walking, its uplifting effect on body and mind and spirit. Like all good things, though, it is open to abuse. There are two types, occasionally encountered in the Lake District, who especially offend me.

The first are those who see the sport as another field for athletic competition and self-assertion. They push past on narrow paths and disappear into the distance, heads down and noticing nothing, apparently intent on getting it all over as quickly as possible. They are invariably male and mercifully few, though you sometimes hear them in the pubs in the evening, boasting of distances covered and times clocked, recommending short cuts that no one in his right mind would wish to take.

The second group consists of the over-officious, self-appointed, Pecksniffian guardians of the Country Code. They are usually male too, and middle-aged. They are easily recognised because they move about in small groups, in a controlled fashion, all very correctly dressed and equipped. They are often members of the Ramblers' Club and make sure you know it. They keep a sharp eye out for all forms of backsliding, and like nothing better than to march up to other walkers and confront them with direct questions: 'What are you doing up here in tennis shoes?' 'Do you think your dog is under proper control?' It is frightening to think what they would have said if they had come across Coleridge with his broom-handle and his knapsack and his hopelessly inadequate map. Fundamentally, of course, their cause is a good one – the fells need protection – but the way they pursue it amounts to a denial of the spirit of the sport, which has always been free and adventurous and friendly.

Coleridge walked in that spirit. He arrived at the pretty village of Nether Wasdale in the early afternoon and sat down to refresh himself and add a further paragraph to his letter to Sara Hutchinson:

> ... So I went on, turned eastward, up the Irt, the Sea behind and Wastdale Mountains before – and here I am – Wed. Afternoon ½ past 3, Augt. 4th. 1802 – Wastdale, a mile and half below the Foot of the Lake, at an Alehouse without a Sign, 20 strides from the Door, under the Shade of a huge Sycamore Tree, without my coat – but that I will now put on, in prudence – yes, here I am, and have been for something more than an hour, and have *enjoyed* a good Dish of Tea (I carried my Tea and sugar with me) under this delightful Tree. In the House there are only an old feeble Woman, and a *'Tallyeur'* Lad upon the Table – all the rest of the Wastdale World is a-haymaking, rejoicing and thanking God for this first downright summer Day that we have had since the beginning of May.

The old pub, now called the Screes, is still there. The 'Tallyeur' would have been a young tailor, staying at the house to run up whatever clothes the family needed. This was common practice in those days in remote places, and the Wasdale Valley is the remotest in the Lake District. I saw no hay-making when I walked through. Presumably it had been done weeks before, in the long dry spell. Most Cumbrian farmers nowadays choose to make silage anyway. It is an easier process; the grass does not have to be dry; and many say the animals prefer it as their winter fodder.

Just outside Nether Wasdale I was passed by a brewer's van, cheerfully emblazoned with the words 'The Flying Pint'. By the roadside there was a small, stone-built shelter. Inside it I found a carved inscription, written in 1923 by Commander Sir Graham Bower of the Royal Navy. It read:

> In reverent memory of the men of all nations who have given their lives in the cause of patriotism and duty and who now rest united in God's peace, the peace of reconciliation and of love and brotherhood to all men of good will by the heralds of the Prince of Peace.

I reflected on the news bulletin I had watched on television the night before, which told of the further destruction of the once splendid city of Beirut; Indian soldiers shooting Tamil people in Sri Lanka; the extremists in Northern Ireland celebrating 20 years of the army on their streets by killing each other and hurling stones.

Coleridge walked on to Wastwater:

> Between the Lake and the Mountains on the left, a low ridge of hill runs parallel with the Lake, for more than half its length; and just at the foot of the Lake there is a Bank, even and smooth and low like a grassy Bank in a Gentleman's Park. Along the hilly Ridge I walked thro' a Lane of green Hazels, with hay-fields and Hay-makers on my Right.... The Lake is wholly hidden 'till your very Feet touch it, as one may say, and to a Stranger the Burst would be almost overwhelming.

Wasdale is the most forbidding of the Lake District valleys. The lake itself is dark and cold. As you advance towards the valley head, high mountains rear up on all sides: Seatallan and Yewbarrow on the left; Great Gable, with its red-tinted screes, directly ahead; Lingmell and the Scafells to the right. Across the lake, you are confronted by the great curtain of what are called 'the Screes' – a steep slope (more than a mile across and 1,500 feet in height) of loose rocks and boulders with even steeper crags above them, unstable in appearance and riven by gullies.

The angle of the slope continues, they say, a further 250 feet below the surface of the water.

Coleridge had seen it before, but was astonished all over again and sat down by the lakeside, his *Notebook* on his knee, to try to capture the scene:

> O what a Lake – I am sitting at the foot almost – for three miles the Screes form its right bank – a facing of naked Rock of enormous height, and two thirds of its height downward absolutely perpendicular, and then slanting off in Screes, steep as the meal out of the Miller's grinding Trough or Spout – but in the middle of the Lake the Screes commence far higher up, and occupy two thirds of the height in the shape of the apron of a sheet of falling water, (or a pointed Decanter, or tumbler turned upside down) or rather an outspread Fan . . . .

In his letter to Sara Hutchinson, he continued his search for the aptest image:

> . . . the Screes, or facing of bare Rock of enormous Height, two thirds of its height downwards absolutely perpendicular; and then slanting off in *Screes*, or Shiver, consisting of fine red Streaks running in broad Stripes thro' a stone colour – slanting off from the Perpendicular, as steep as the meal newly ground from the Miller's spout. So it is at the foot of the Lake; but higher up this streaky Shiver occupies two thirds of the whole height, like a pointed Decanter in shape, or an outspread Fan, or a long-waisted old maid with a fine prim apron, or – no, other things that would only fill up the Paper.

Almost everyone stops at this point to gaze across the lake to the vast curtain of the Screes. Nowadays most people simply take out their cameras and record the scene on film. But there have been many writers too, and most of them have attempted some kind of description. I have read none so apt and vivid as these lines hurriedly scribbled by Coleridge.

He walked along the northern shores of the lake, where the narrow road now runs. I knew this bit of the route well so I decided to do something I had not done before and follow the path at the foot of the Screes. It is very pleasant going at first – through the grounds of Wasdale Hall which is now a youth hostel, then along the lakeside by a gravelly, tree-rooty path. There were frequent light showers but the trees sheltered me on this stretch. A wooden bridge spans the River Irt, where it begins its short journey to the sea. Here the path turns to the north-east but continues to be enjoyable for a while. Then, quite suddenly, you come to a wide and vicious band of broken boulders, jumbled crazily together on the steep slope immediately above the lake. The path disappears. You have to take your hands out of your pockets and scramble across carefully. Some of the stones move and wobble when you put your weight on them. All of them were wet and slippery from the recent rain.

I was about one-third of the way across when I saw a middle-aged man making his way towards me. He was clearly agitated and, when he could make himself heard, shouted up: 'My friend's fallen and knocked himself unconscious. He's about five minutes further on, a bit lower down. There are two women with him – our wives. I'm going to get the Mountain Rescue.' I said I would find them and see what I could do, and he scurried off.

In a few minutes I found the little group, crouched among the boulders. The injured man's head was caked in blood but he had come round and was talking articulately. It was raining lightly, and the women had wrapped him up in spare clothing and covered him with a plastic sheet. The two couples were friends from Barrow-in-Furness, out for a day's walking in the fells. I gave the man my last bar of chocolate and soon after he sat up and said he felt fit enough to make his own way along. We managed to dissuade him. Two young men rowed close inshore, 50 feet below us, and asked if they could help by ferrying him across the lake, but we declined the offer, saying the Mountain Rescue people were coming.

I stayed with them for half an hour but there was nothing

further I could do so I said I would go on to Wasdale Head and make sure the rescue team were on the way. By this time the sun was shining again. I moved, very gingerly, across the boulders, and before long came to a good path through the bracken, with dramatic views of the scree slopes above and the shattered crags above them. A yellow Mountain Rescue helicopter passed low overhead, looking for the scene of the accident. Expert help was on the way.

There are now 14 Mountain Rescue teams in the Lake District and the surrounding area. Each has between 30 and 50 volunteer members, men and women, ready to turn out at any time of the day or night. They are amateur in the sense that they get no pay, but very professional in their approach to the job. They are trained in first aid and hold regular practice sessions, rehearsing techniques and skills – radio communication, abseiling, night searches with trained dogs, lowering stretcher cases down vertical cliffs. They have specialised medical and climbing equipment, walkie-talkie radios, Land Rovers and the power to summon a helicopter. In an average year they are called out about 200 times.

Organised mountain rescue did not emerge in the Lake District until after the Second World War. Before that, if someone went missing in the mountains, some kind of search operation would be mounted, usually involving the local policeman, one or two shepherds, any fell-walkers who would help and, if possible, a doctor. In Coleridge's day there was no system at all, and there were very few people about in the hills. Had he fallen and injured himself so badly that he could not walk or crawl down to the valley, Coleridge would almost certainly have died of thirst or exposure before anyone found him. He knew that but did not allow the thought to deter him.

Wasdale Head is less changed than any of the other valleys Coleridge visited. There is a hotel there now and a car park, and, during the holiday season, there are usually many tents in the roadside fields. Otherwise, it looks much the same as it has done for centuries – embowered, almost encircled by high mountains, the meeting place of two sparkling streams. In his *Guide to the Lakes* Wordsworth spoke of '... the deep valley of

Wastdale, with its little chapel, and half a dozen neat dwellings scattered upon a plain meadow and corn-ground, intersected with stone walls apparently innumerable, like a large piece of lawless patchwork'. The description still stands.

William Hutchinson, writing more than 20 years before Wordsworth, took a more personal and moralistic approach:

> Wasdale Head is a narrow dale, the inclosures small and irregular, but level, divided with stone walls; the village chiefly inhabited by shepherds; upon the whole, this scene is exceedingly wild and sequestered, but to the contemplative person, who is a lover of romantic views, these places have a thousand beauties.... The inhabitants of these distant dales are blunt, simple and honest; neither science nor fraud have yet got much footing there; so that innocence and happiness may be presumed to prevail: but alas! is it not to be feared, that the passions of envy, hatred and malice, so natural to man, in his primeval and most uncultivated state, may not, in a great measure, disturb those blessings!

Hutchinson also gives factual information about Wasdale Head at the end of the eighteenth century. There were, he says, 3,000 Herdwick sheep grazing the valley fields and the common ground of the higher fells. The only grain that would grow there was oats, and there was not much of that. The lake and rivers were rich in trout and eels and some char; one trout caught in Wastwater weighed 12 pounds. High up in the mountains there were many wild cats, foxes and martens. In earlier times red squirrels had been plentiful but the felling of the woods had driven most of them out. The big predatory birds – eagles, falcons, ravens – had been driven away as well. Hutchinson described the air as 'clear and salubrious'; the water as 'remarkably transparent and light'. As a result, the inhabitants were 'hale and hearty', but there were fewer of them than formerly:

> Though the common right at Wasdale Head is very extensive, affording pasturage for large flocks of sheep, yet the valley is thinly inhabited, and very confined,

containing, as it is computed, little more than a mile in length. The village contains eight families, three of land owners, four farmers, and one labourer, in all 47 inhabitants; there is no mill, public house, shop or tradesman in the valley, notwithstanding it is a considerable distance from any market-town.

The valley head has four traditional claims to fame: England's highest mountain, Scafell Pike; its deepest lake; the smallest church; and the biggest liar. The biggest liar was Will Ritson, the dominant figure in this region in the last century. They called him 'the King o' Wasdale'. A nearby waterfall is named after him, and so is the bar of the hotel – his portrait hangs as an inn sign over the entrance. This is entirely appropriate as he was a great drinker and it was he who opened the first pub in the area. In 1856 he added a small wing on the end of his farmhouse, got a drinks licence and called it the Huntsman's Inn. It quickly became the local social centre – for the menfolk. And visitors from much further afield were soon coming to stay, to see the unique valley head and enjoy 'Auld Will Ritson's' company and conversation.

'Crack' is the dialect word for this kind of relaxed talking, the exchange – usually accompanied by drinking – of ideas and jokes and old stories. It is still a popular Cumbrian pastime, conducted in a rich, dipthong-laden dialect that can make the talk of the locals virtually impenetrable to outsiders. It is not only the strangeness of the sound – many of the words they use cannot be found in the *Oxford English Dictionary*. This was Ritson's language. Many of his remarks and stories have been handed down and, although he made no vocal concessions to his 'offcomer' visitors, it is possible, with a little effort, to understand his meaning. The effort is worthwhile.

Ritson was not a monologuist in the Coleridge manner. He liked the give and take of convivial chat. But there was a competitive edge in it too. He had an incomparable fund of stories about local characters, a sharp eye for human frailty, a ready wit, and a fine line in high-flying fantasy. They held an annual contest in Wasdale (they still do) to find who could tell the tallest story, and Ritson won it year after year. One of his prize-winning tales concerned a male eagle who badly damaged one wing and was brought down to a farm to be nursed by a fox-hound bitch. After a while, feeling better, the eagle took advantage of his nurse. The outcome was a baby fox-hound with the wings of an eagle, an incomparable hunter, able to cruise along the screes and cliffs in pursuit of its prey. He would deliver these fantasies with a deadpan expression and much circumstantial detail. But he won the competition one year, it is said, with a single laconic statement: 'I canna compete this year because I canna tell a lee.'

An early visitor to the Huntsman's Inn was the Lancashire poet Edwin Waugh who was pinned down there by a violent storm and spent a whole day listening to the 'crack' in the kitchen:

> I was most interested in Ritson's anecdotes of famous men who had visited Wasdale. He had wandered many a day with Professor Wilson, Wordsworth, Professor Sedgwick, De Quincey and others. He spoke of Words-worth as 'a varra quiet-like aad man, who had nea pride aboot him, an' varra lile to say'. But Professor Wilson 'banged 'em all for fun'. Ritson had been a famous wrestler in his youth, and had won many a country belt in Cumberland. He once wrestled with Wilson, and threw him twice out of three falls. But he owned that the professor was 'a varray bad un to lick'.

This was Professor John Wilson of Elleray, near Winder-mere, a flamboyant, larger-than-life figure. Although Scottish in origin, he claims a prominent place in the list of Cumbrian eccentrics. More than anyone else, he spanned all of Lakeland life. He competed in the local sports meetings, challenged the valley champions, and cheerfully presented prizes to them when he was beaten. He loved cock-fighting so much that he had his dining room floor laid with turf so that he and his friends could enjoy 'the mains' without bothering to go out. He was a frequent visitor to Wasdale Head, sailing and fishing on the lake, wrest-ling Will Ritson and engaging in other athletic contests, talking the night through in the little bar at the Huntsman's Inn.

But he was equally at home in the drawing rooms of what passed for 'genteel society' – the squires and their ladies; wealthy offcomers who had built themselves holiday retreats in the valleys; the growing band of cultured people, artists and writers, who were settling in the District.

John Wilson seemed to have everything, in unfair measure: good looks, vitality, athletic ability, courage, charm, a sharp mind and a highly articulate tongue, independent means, a high sense of fun, an open and generous spirit. He was educated at Glasgow University, then at Oxford. In 1807 he settled into the house he had built at Elleray, and hurled himself into the life of the District. He was soon great friends with the Wordsworth family, and especially with Thomas De Quincey. He won the hand of the local beauty. When he lost his fortune, through no fault of his own, he went to Edinburgh and became a very successful journalist and author. Later, through political dexterity, he was appointed Professor of Moral Philosophy at Edinburgh University, though he knew nothing about the subject and had to get friends (De Quincey among them) to help him write his lectures.

He was something of a conman, but undoubtedly an engaging and accomplished one. It is a tribute to the impact of his personality that he succeeded in charming Miss Harriet Martineau of Ambleside, the sharp-eyed and formidable writer and economist. She writes about Professor Wilson almost as if she were in love with him. 'He made others happy,' she said, 'by being so intensely happy himself'.

But he did not charm Coleridge. As in the case of John Hatfield, the 'Keswick Imposter' who bigamously married the 'Beauty of Buttermere', Coleridge was not to be persuaded by superficial allure. He met Wilson briefly in Grasmere in 1810, when both were guests of the Wordsworths, and dismissed him as 'a silly Wordsworth-idolator' (as opposed to being a sensible 'Wordsworth-honourer'). Anyone today who succeeds in reading Wilson's essays – rhetorical and rhapsodical, full of high-flown sentiments that ring very false – will probably incline towards Coleridge's judgement.

Pieter van Dyke's portrait of Coleridge, painted in 1795. The year after, Coleridge described himself in a letter: ''Tis a mere carcase of a face; fat, flabby and expressive chiefly of inexpression'. But those who knew him said that the moment he began talking his face became very animated indeed.

This silhouette (made in 1827, when she was 52) is the only known portrait of Sara Hutchinson, with whom Coleridge was hopelessly in love for many years and to whom he wrote the letters describing his long fell-walk.

Greta Hall which was Coleridge's home in Keswick for three and a half years and that of his brother-in-law Robert Southey for nearly 40 years.

Gees

Egremont

Cold Fell

Hardhow

Copeland

4.

Keswick

Buttermere

Derwent Copills Forest

Red Pike

Beckermouth

Ennerdale

Calder

Gailter Calder

Steeple

River Calder

Blaieng & P. Fells

Pillar

Bolton Wood

Herscirk

Keswick Crag

Black Lea Windmore

Bonewood

Seatallian

Gos forth

Wastdale

Dring

King Camb

Melbreachy

Screes

Ghyhead

Sea Fell

Waberthwaite

miterdale

Ravenglass

Black House

Bowfell

Sea

Eskdale

Rows to Kendall

Hardknott

Devoch

Corney Fell

Annes View Fell

Black Coab

V. Parlur

Coniston

Dead Man Bridge

... House on Sunday morning, August 1. 1802
... the bridge by the Ross Skiddaw to my right,
... harbour of Borrodale mountains behind me,
... lands Rock of the 3 M. within it, to my
... Second Inclosure, view of Vicarage.
... views of the Bridge / when you come into
... Road Castlerigg lying flat upon Skiddaw,
... in a Pantry / the Bridge / view at the
... roemakers in Portinscale / the Trunk of Oak
... pretty view over the Peak — the grand
... view in the Top of the Hill —

... in side, the grand view, — to the Right
... to the left at the lake / ... Bridge
... lands, general character of houses
... below the road, liveliness of the vale /
... wildness of the Fells — yet even there
... finest plants softened down by the
... circular lines of bason-like
... concavities — Akein. Eich. hayn /
... no doubt in a throng
... extravagantly exaggerated by Werth /
... Buttermere / the mere in
... what a singular Embracement
... of naked Rock / exactly an enormous
... the Bason, of which one half is
... gone / Ascent by Scale force / going
... a level — ruspy roff ground / every
... man his own path-maker —
... skin of gauze — when rushes
... grow, a man may go
... Peter peeps in one you
... left / on the right

(Left) Coleridge copied this rough map of western Cumberland into his *Notebook* from the map in William Hutchinson's *History and Antiquities of Cumberland* (1794). It was his only navigational aid on the 'circumcursion'. The dotted line indicates the route he meant to take and makes it clear that he originally intended to return home by way of Wasdale, Sty Head Pass and Borrowdale. (Right) The beginning of Coleridge's *Notebook* account of his nine-day walk. The passage begins: 'Quitted my House on Sunday morning, August 1 1802 over the bridge by the Hops/Skiddaw to my right, upper halves of Borrodale mountains behind me . . .'

In Coleridge's day, what he called 'the Prospect Bridge at Portinscale' carried the main road from Keswick across the River Derwent and then on to Cockermouth and the west coast.

Now the river is spanned by a metal suspension bridge which carries pedestrians only. The ancient stone bridge was irreparably damaged by flood waters in 1954.

Coleridge spent the first night of his walk at Long Moor Farm, near Ennerdale Bridge. The front of the building – apart from the fence and a brutal wall dividing the garden – looks much the same as it did when Coleridge was there, when it was only ten years old. It is no longer a farm, and has been split to form two private houses.

The front of Taw House Farm in the Eskdale Valley. The stone above the door gives 1789 as the date of building. Apart from some weathering, the only apparent change is the satellite television dish.

This is what Ennerdale Valley looked like, from the upper slopes of Great Gable, in the years before the Forestry Commission began planting. Pillar Mountain dominates the left skyline, with a corner of Ennerdale Lake peeping over its shoulder. The lake on the right is Crummock Water.

Ennerdale Valley as it appears today, with its vast conifer plantations.

Mickledore Gap separates Scafell from Scafell Pike. The steep, broken ground beyond the narrow ridge is Broad Stand, the route which Coleridge followed in his exciting descent from the summit of Scafell.

The handsome cirque of mountains at the head of Eskdale, seen from near the site of the Roman fort on Hardknott Pass. Ill Crag (near Scafell Pike) is on the left skyline; Esk Pike in the centre; Bow Fell on the right.

This is what Thirlmere looked like, from the south, in the years before Manchester got permission to turn the lake into a reservoir.

The same valley, from much the same view-point, today.

All this, however, was in the future when Coleridge made his way to the furthest farm at Wasdale Head in the late afternoon of 4th August 1802:

> ... and so on to Kirk Fell, at the foot of which is Thomas Tyson's House where Wordsworth and I slept Novr. will be 3 years – and there I was welcomed kindly, had a good Bed, and left it after Breakfast.

The farm where he stayed, Burnthwaite, is still there: a long, low jumble of old stone buildings set among trees and a maze of dry-stone walls. It is very much a working farm, chiefly sheep. One or two barns may have been added in the past two centuries but it looks much as it must have done to Coleridge. They still accommodate visitors, but it was full when I called so I made my way back along the path, crossing a wooden bridge over the beck, to find a room at Middle Row, next to the Wastwater Hotel. At least it meant I had not so far to walk to get a steak and kidney pie and a couple of pints in the Ritson bar.

The hotel makes a point of honouring its past, with many fine old photographs of rock-climbers and others on its walls.

More than any other valley head in the Lake District, that of Wasdale makes you simultaneously aware of mutability and permanence. The spirits of those who lived and worked and played there seem all around. But you are surrounded, too, by great symbols of changelessness – the majestic mountains and rushing waters, the dark depths of the lake, the astonishing screes. It is a place of many moods, all of them powerful. In some of the other valleys man has taken over and imposed himself on the landscape indelibly. At Wasdale Head, even when there are many people about, man still seems small, transient and largely ineffectual. It is the starkest of all the valleys, and the strongest, and the most impressively mysterious.

CHAPTER SEVEN

Mountain Adventure

Thursday 5th August 1802 was the fifth day of Coleridge's 'circumcursion' and it marked, in more than one way, the high point of his long walk. It was literally the high point, since he reached the summit of Scafell, 3,162 feet above sea level, the second-highest point of land in England. It is a splendid, craggy top, commanding superb and varied views, and Coleridge's spirits soared. Characteristically, he descended by way of a short cut called Broad Stand which is nowadays regarded as a route for climbers, not walkers. The adventure excited and exhilarated him. His detailed account of the day, in his letters to Sara Hutchinson, covers five full pages – in the printed version – much more than he devoted to any other day of the walk.

The entry in his *Notebook* begins with these words:

> Thursday Morning, August 5, 1802 left T. Tyson's at Wastdale Head where I had been most hospitably entertained, and had an excellent Bed, moved down the vale almost to the Lake head, and ascended in the low reach between the Screes and Sca fell, and in about a mile came in sight of Burnmoor Tairn, a pretty piece of water flounder-shaped, lying just under the back of the Screes, a gap and inverted arch at its head, with Black Comb and a peep of the Sea, its Tail towards Scafell, which I am now ascending, and wrote this on the side of the Hill, down which two Becks fall over stones and precipices and join when they reach the level – I am sitting by the Eskdale side – O for wealth to *wood* these Tarns – Weeping Birches with Mountain Ash and Laburnum, with Hollies for underwood....

The original woods had been chopped down and it is interesting that Coleridge would have liked to replant the area, not with larch and spruce, but with a variety of broadleaf trees and shrubs.

Within minutes of leaving Burnthwaite Farm he must have walked past the little chapel but, true to his custom, he went straight on. In those days there was no burial ground here, and the bodies of Wasdale Head folk had to be carted 6 miles or more over the fell, past Burnmoor Tarn by what was called 'the old corpse road', to be buried at the church in Eskdale. Today there is a graveyard at Wasdale Head and it holds many sad reminders of the price that some rock-climbers and mountaineers have had to pay for the pleasures of their sport. Saddest of all is the spot where three young men lie alongside each other, all killed – with a fourth, who is buried elsewhere – when they fell from the Pinnacle Face of Scafell in September 1903. It was the first fatal accident in Lake District rock-climbing, which is a remarkable fact when you consider that the sport had been actively pursued for more than 20 years by that time, moving on to ever more difficult and dangerous routes with equipment and safety techniques that were little short of suicidal. The four young men who died at the foot of Scafell Pinnacle wore stout country boots, heavily nailed in the soles and heels, and were joined together by short lengths of hemp rope. That was all they had for protection. But none of them had taken the precaution – basic now in the sport – of tying himself to the rock so that he could not be pulled off. As a result, when the leader slipped, the others were pulled to their deaths.

It was no accident that Wasdale Head became the birthplace of rock-climbing. It lies within easy reach of many challenging cliffs, all composed of the durable and – on the whole – reliable rock called Borrowdale Volcanic: Pillar Rock; two faces of Great Gable and one of Green Gable; Scafell Crag, the biggest expanse of steep rock in England; and other inviting outcrops. In the 1880s, when the first community of climbers evolved, the valley head was even more remote than it is today. Visitors had to walk the 8 miles from the railway station on the coast, or hire a coach to convey themselves and their luggage. The pioneer climbers preferred it that way. They liked the savagery and privacy of Wasdale Head. They did not want to be watched by crowds of tourists as they struggled up their new routes.

There was another important factor. By this time Ritson's little annex bar had grown into a proper hotel. Ritson retired in 1879, and his place was taken by Dan Tyson (no relation to Thomas Tyson) who extended the building considerably and changed its name to the Wastwater Hotel. For many years it was the headquarters of the rock-climbers. At Christmas, Easter and Whitsun it was entirely taken over by the 'cragsmen' as they called themselves. 'The place,' one of them said, 'stank of drying tweeds.'

They were a high-spirited, convivial crowd, exclusively male, in their twenties and thirties, nearly all of them well-educated and well-heeled. They came from the big cities – London, Manchester, Liverpool, Bradford – and belonged to the professional middle class. They were teachers, engineers, businessmen, doctors and lawyers – most of them university men who were now comfortably embarked on their careers. But they wanted more than material comfort. They needed, occasionally, to get away from the city smoke and the routines and restrictions of their working and domestic lives, to stretch mind and body in demanding situations and in congenial company.

A few local men were attracted to the sport, but most of them thought it was a crazy way of enjoying yourself. Will Ritson was a great fell-walker but could not understand the craze for climbing: 'What's makkin' ye fellas fash yer'sels seea mich aboot climmin' t' crags?' he demanded. 'Isn't t' fells big eneugh for ye?' Dan Tyson, although he made his climbing customers very welcome, said they were 'daft', and when he first saw one of them with 'an Alpine rope' over his shoulder, wanted to know 'if theer was gaahn to be a hangin' job on?'

Despite this, and the continued bewilderment of the great majority of folk, the sport has flourished and spread and changed almost beyond recognition. Today there are tens of thousands across the developed world who practise rock-climbing. Many of them are addicted to it. It is no longer for men only; not confined to the young; by no means exclusive to the educated middle class. Since the Second World War there have been major advances in equipment and safety techniques, and they have proved so effective that – though climbing still looks dangerous and still feels exciting – its casualty rate is low for a danger sport. It was not always so. The pioneers' fundamental law was that 'the leader must not fall', but it was a rule that was easier to pronounce than to observe. The first half of this century saw many serious accidents on the Lake District crags, as the graveyard at Wasdale Head testifies.

Among the graves there is one of a man who, although a keen climber, was not killed climbing. His headstone says simply: 'A. P. Rossiter – Climber in these hills. 1903–1957'. He is worth noting as we pass by because he was the first person, as far as I can discover, who wrote with a full and acute appreciation about Coleridge's innovative response to the wild landscape of the District.

Rossiter was a student of English literature who became a Fellow of Jesus College, Cambridge, in 1945 and held the post until his death. Coleridge had studied at Jesus College. Perhaps it was this, as well as the fact that the college has a splendid portrait of Coleridge by James Northcote, that inspired him to study the unpublished *Notebooks* (most of them in the British Museum) as well as the poems and letters. Once he started his research, he was captivated. In 1951 he wrote to Kathleen Coburn, a Canadian scholar who had published studies of Coleridge's writings:

> ... I am a Cambridge don and a rock-climber, with a literary-critical interest in the development of aesthetic attitudes towards mountains between the late 17th century and the 19th, and for some years I have made a practice of going and seeing – or trying to see – the places which are described in Gray's *Journal*, Gilpin, West's *Guide* (1776) and so on. Consequently I was extremely interested by Coleridge on Scafell ...

Miss Coburn was already preparing Coleridge's *Notebooks* for publication and promptly enlisted Rossiter's help in dealing with the passages about his time in the Lake District. He worked with great assiduity. And the fruits of his researches are apparent in the volume of *Notes* to Volume One of the published *Notebooks*, which came out a few months after his death in a motor accident.

Unfortunately Rossiter published very little. The chief thing seems to be an article, only a few pages long, in the 1954 edition of the Journal of the Fell and Rock Climbing Club of the English Lake District. In it, he said:

> Whether you care about Coleridge or not, it is often illuminating to see what could be noticed in, and felt about, so inexhaustible a part of England some 150 years ago, when its secrets were the prerogative of a few; and the more illuminating when it comes from the spontaneous jottings, in notebook or letter, of a man with the gift of words, and, besides that, some slight claim to be called the earliest of English rock-scramblers.... No writer has more often or more sensitively recorded the effects of sun and cloud, the unanticipated beauties of rain and storm, and the evanescent panoramas of the night-sky.

When Rossiter was a student at Cambridge his tutor had been I. A. Richards, remembered now as a formative literary critic and protagonist of Basic English. Richards was also deeply interested in Coleridge and, in his younger days, had been a leading rock-climber, mostly on the cliffs of Snowdonia.

I thought of these scholars, and the fascination which Coleridge held for them and for many others, as I made my way past the church and the campsite, across the river, and up the path that leads to Burnmoor Tarn. Early that morning there had been some heavy showers and, although it was clear again for the moment, the path was still running with water in places. The high summits around were blanketed by grey clouds. I hoped, without great confidence, that they would disperse before I reached them. Just before the tarn, I turned left to cross swampy ground and begin the steeper ascent, to the left of Hardrigg Gill, that leads to Green How and then to Scafell summit.

As Coleridge ascended, his mind was filled with wild ideas

and fantasies. He recorded them in his *Notebook*, hoping they might come in useful some time:

> A gentle Madman that would wander still over the Mountains by the lonely Tairns – the like never seen since the crazy Shepherd, who having lost almost all his sheep in the long hard snow was repulsed or thought himself coldly treated by his Sweet-heart – and so went a wanderer seeking his Sheep for ever, in storm and snow especially .... my Peter Pounce who had just come from the Moon, 8 miles high, volcanos – people wear asbestos, and wash themselves in liquid Storax – Have their fire conducted into their house by great stone pipes as we have water....
>
> Bear witness for me, what thoughts I wandered about with – if ever I imagined myself a conqueror, it was always to bring peace – but mostly turned away from these thoughts to more humane and peaceable Dreams ...

He stopped twice to scribble these notes, and list the mountains and moors and streams he could see all round him. It is a steep but delightful path most of the way, a mixture of rock and grass and lovely mosses, though the final 200 feet are very badly eroded. At one point, about two-thirds of the way up, I moved over to the left to look down on Wasdale Head and westwards to the coast and the steaming towers of Sellafield. The cloud, immediately above me now, had not dispersed.

In his letter to Sara, Coleridge said nothing of the 'wild activity of thoughts, imaginations, feelings and impulses of motion' that had crowded his mind on the way up. It was early afternoon when he reached the summit. He stayed there a considerable time, admiring the situation and the views in all directions and continuing his letter:

> I ascended Sca'Fell by the side of a torrent, and climbed and rested, rested and climbed, 'till I gained the very summit of Sca'Fell – believed by the Shepherds here to be higher than either Helvellyn or Skiddaw .... O

my God! what enormous Mountains these are close by me, and yet below the Hill I stand on – Great Gavel, Kirk Fell, Green Crag, and behind the Pillar, then the Steeple, then the Hay Cock. . . . And here I am *lounded* [a Cumberland dialect word that meant 'sheltered'] – so fully lounded that tho' the wind is strong, and the clouds are hastening hither from the Sea – and the whole air seaward has a lurid look – and we shall certainly have Thunder – yet here (but that I am hunger'd and provisionless) *here* I could lie warm, and wait methinks for tomorrow's Sun, and on a nice Stone Table am I now at this moment writing to you – between 2 and 3 o'Clock as I guess, surely the first Letter ever written from the top of Sca'Fell.

The weather, at this stage, was better for Coleridge than it was for me. It was chilly on top when I arrived and there were no views at all. It is a spacious summit with incomparable rock scenery at its northern edge, but this, too, was hidden. The cloud was thick. Visibility was not more than 10 yards and I had some trouble finding the summit cairn. I was casting about for it when I came across six teenagers, three lads and three girls, who had come up by the steep West Wall Traverse and were determined not to go back that way.

Coleridge must have settled himself at the northern edge of the summit plateau, immediately above the soaring walls and gullies of Scafell Crag where, 80 years later, the pioneer rock-climbers were to start their explorations:

But O! what a look down just under my Feet! The frightfullest Cove that might ever be seen, huge perpendicular Precipices, and one Sheep upon it's only Ledge, that surely must be crag! Tyson told me of this place, and called it Hollow Stones. Just by it and joining together, rise two huge Pillars of bare lead-coloured stone – I am no measurer, but their height and depth is terrible. I know how unfair it is to judge of these Things by a comparison of past Impressions with present – but I have no shadow of hesitation in

> saying that the Coves and Precipices of Helvellyn are
> nothing to these! But from this sweet lounding Place
> I see directly thro' Borrowdale, the Castle Crag, the
> whole of Derwent Water, and but for the haziness of
> the Air I could see my own House – I see clear enough
> where it stands.

The thought of Greta Hall did not, it seems, bring his family to
mind. If it did, he made no mention of them either in the letter
or in his *Notebook*.

He concluded:

> Here I will fold up this Letter – I have Wafers in my
> Inkhorn, and you shall call this Letter when it passes
> before you the Sca'Fell Letter – I must now drop down,
> how I may into Eskdale – that lies under to my right –
> the upper part of it the wildest and savagest surely of
> all the Vales that were ever seen from the Top of an
> English Mountain and the lowest part the loveliest.

He descended to the Mickledore Gap, between Scafell and
Scafell Pike, by way of Broad Stand. Some have claimed that he
may have gone down by a nearby route called Mickledore
Chimney, but Coleridge's detailed account, allowing for a
certain amount of understandable exaggeration, fits Broad Stand
much more closely. A. P. Rossiter was sure it was Broad Stand
and so am I.

Wainwright, in his *Pictorial Guide to the Southern Fells*,
firmly instructs all walkers to resist any temptation to tackle
this route: 'The author first made this resolve in 1930 and has
repeated it a score of times since then; his continuing disappointment is amply compensated by the pleasure of going on
living'. There is one awkward move, about 30 feet up, and a
fall there could have, indeed has had, very serious and sometimes
fatal consequences. The route is listed in the climbers' guides,
though it gets the lowest possible grading – 'Moderate'.

At this point, I have a confession to make. I had arranged
for a young friend, who is a capable climber, to meet me on the
summit of Scafell. When I finally located the cairn, he was there,

waiting patiently. He had brought his climbing rope with him.
He had come up via Broad Stand and reported that the rock
was very wet and, although he had looked carefully, he had not
been able to find a place where he could tie himself securely to
the crag so that he might fully protect my descent. I thought
about it, but not for long. 'We'll go down by Foxes Tarn,' I
said, taking the much safer option.

It was breaking my rule about doing the walk as exactly in
Coleridge's footsteps as possible, and I can only plead two
arguments in mitigation. In the first place, had I slipped and
killed myself on the awkward move, this book would never have
been written. In the second, I had already done the descent of
Broad Stand in the Coleridge way, alone, without the protection
of a rope. I had done it many years before, when I was climbing
regularly and was much younger and suppler and more confident, and also when the rock was reassuringly dry.

Even so, I felt slightly guilty as we set off to find the easier
way down. Coleridge, after all, had gone boldly on, to tackle
what was unknown ground to him. He was completely alone;
he saw no one all that day until he reached the Eskdale valley.
He described the adventure the next morning, starting the second
part of his Scafell Letter to Sara Hutchinson:

> There is one sort of Gambling, to which I am much
> addicted; and that is not of the least criminal kind for
> a man who has children and a Concern. It is this.
> When I find it convenient to descend from a mountain,
> I am too confident and too indolent to look round
> about and wind about 'till I find a track or other
> symptom of safety; but I wander on, and where it is
> first *possible* to descend, there I go – relying upon
> fortune for how far down this possibility will continue.
> So it was yesterday afternoon.... the first place I came
> to, that was not direct Rock, I slipped down, and went
> on for a while with tolerable ease – but now I came
> (it was midway down) to a smooth perpendicular rock
> about 7 feet high – this was nothing – I put my hands
> on the ledge and dropped down – in a few yards came

just such another – I *dropped* that too, and yet another, seemed not higher – I would not stand for a trifle so I dropped that too – but the stretching of the muscles of my hands and arms, and the jolt of the Fall on my Feet, put my whole Limbs in a *Tremble*, and I paused, and looking down, saw that I had little else to encounter but a succession of these little Precipices – it was in truth a Path that in a very hard Rain is, no doubt, the channel of a most splendid Waterfall. So I began to suspect that I ought not to go on, but then unfortunately tho' I could with ease drop down a smooth Rock 7 feet high, I could not *climb* it, so go on I must and on I went. . . .

All climbers will recognise the dilemma. Many excellent new routes have been made by leaders who, however unsure they may feel of finding a manageable way ahead, are quite sure they cannot retrace the steps already taken. No climber today, however, would tackle the descent of Broad Stand in the Coleridge style, hanging by his fingers and dropping down to the ledge below. His pell-mell description – it covers three printed pages without a single paragraph break – goes on:

. . . the next 3 drops were not half a Foot, at least not a foot more than my own height, but every Drop increased the Palsy of my Limbs – I shook all over, Heaven knows without the least influence of Fear, and now I had only two more to drop down, to return was impossible – but of these two the first was tremendous, it was twice my own height, and the Ledge at the bottom was so exceedingly narrow, that if I dropt down upon it I must of necessity have fallen backwards and of course killed myself. My Limbs were all in a tremble – I lay upon my Back to rest myself, and was beginning according to my Custom to laugh at myself for a Madman, when the sight of the Crags above me on each side, and the impetuous Clouds just over them, posting so luridly and so rapidly northward, overawed me. I lay in a state of almost prophetic Trance and

Delight – and blessed God aloud, for the powers of Reason and the Will, which remaining no Danger can overpower us!

The last line could stand as the fundamental rule for climbers. The vital quality is confidence, but it must be a cool confidence, based on 'the powers of Reason and the Will'. If you let the hazards of the position overwhelm you and give way to desperation and panic, disaster is likely. If you do as Coleridge did – rest awhile and compose yourself, muscles and mind; and stay calm – you will find a safe way past the impending difficulties. It reminds me of something that a veteran Lake District climber – he was past 80 and still climbing – said to me some years ago. We were talking about a route on Great Gable, Eagle's Nest Ridge Direct, which was first climbed in 1892 but which is still graded 'Very Severe'. It is only 120 feet but it is steep and the holds are small and delicate. The old climber had done it many times, always with delight. 'I always think of it,' he said, 'as a great test of one's serenity.'

Coleridge regained his serenity:

O God, I exclaimed aloud – how calm, how blessed am I now – I know not how to proceed, how to return, but I am calm and fearless and confident – if this Reality were a Dream, if I were asleep, what agonies had I suffered! what screams! When the Reason and the Will are away, what remain to us but Darkness and Dimness and a bewildering Shame and Pain that is utterly Lord over us, or fantastic Pleasure, that draws the Soul along swimming through the air in many shapes, even as a Flight of Starlings in a Wind.

The image of a flock of starlings swinging about in the windy sky was a recurring one with Coleridge. At the end of November 1799, returning by coach to London after the northern visit when he saw the Lake District for the first time and fell in love with Sara Hutchinson, he wrote in his *Notebook*:

Starlings in vast flights drove along like smoke, mist or anything misty without volition – now a circular area inclined in an arc – now a globe – now from a complete orb into an elipse and oblong – now a balloon with the car suspended, now a concaved semi-circle – and still it expands and condenses, some moments glimmering and shivering, dim and shadowy, now thickening, deepening, blackening!

In a sense, this is the reverse of the other image that held Coleridge's fascinated interest, that of the waterfall. In the waterfall he found metaphysical meaning because, though the component parts are continually changing, the overall pattern remains constant. With the wheeling birds in the sky, the components stay the same and the pattern constantly changes.

After his long rest on the ledge, Colerige tackled the chief obstacle between him and the path below, the drop he described as 'tremendous' and 'twice my own height'. Infuriatingly, he does not say how he did it. One can only assume he did what he had done so far – hung down by his fingertips and then let go, hoping to maintain his footing on the sloping ledge beneath.

The letter goes on:

I arose, and looking down saw at the bottom a heap of Stones – which had fallen abroad – and rendered the narrow Ledge on which they had been piled, doubly dangerous – at the bottom of the third Rock that I dropt from, I met a dead Sheep quite rotten – This heap of Stones, I guessed, and have since found that I guessed aright, had been piled up by the Shepherd to enable him to climb up and free the poor creature whom he had observed to be crag-fast – but seeing nothing but rock over rock, he had desisted and gone for help – and in the meantime the poor creature had fallen down and killed itself. As I was looking at these I glanced my eye to my left, and observed that the Rock was rent from top to bottom – I measured the breadth of the Rent, and found that there was no danger of my being *wedged* in, so I put my Knap-sack round to my side, and slipped down as between two walls, without any danger or difficulty....

He had reached safe ground, Mickledore Gap. He found the besom-stick which he had thrown down at the start of the rock descent so he could use both hands for climbing. The storm clouds he had seen approaching from the west were now, in his words, 'coming in most tumultuously', so he immediately set off down the steep track to Eskdale, in a state of exhilaration. He noticed a strange physical reaction:

> ... so I began to descend, when I felt an odd sensation across my whole Breast – not pain nor itching – and putting my hand on it found it all bumpy – and on looking saw the whole of my Breast from my Neck to my Navel – and exactly all that my Kamell-hair Breast-shield covers, filled with great red heat-bumps, so thick that no hair could lie between them. They still remain but are evidently less – and I have no doubt will wholly disappear in a few Days. It was however a startling proof to me of the violent exertions which I had made.

I had always assumed, like Coleridge, that it was his exertions that brought on the 'heat-bumps', but a doctor friend tells me they are much more likely to have been caused by something he ate for breakfast, an allergic condition called hives.

There is no doubt that Coleridge had in him the stuff that makes a rock-climber – the boldness and independence, the urge to explore, a head for heights and a good sense of balance. He even understood some of the basic principles. In a *Notebook* entry in September 1800 he said: 'Catch hold of the Bough, as you climb not to sustain but balance'. Clearly he had been tree-climbing rather than rock-climbing but the principle holds for both; the hands and arms tire more easily, so the prudent climber uses them, as far as possible, just to keep himself in balance and lets his legs do the hard lifting work.

Two weeks after he completed the 'circumcursion' Coleridge went, after a heavy downpour, to Moss Force, the waterfall near the top of the Newlands Pass, to see it in spate and to scramble up to the top. He wrote to Sara Hutchinson:

... I soon arrived at the Halse [the Pass] – and climbed up by the waterfall as near as I could, to the very top of the Fell – but it was so craggy – the crags covered with spongy soaky Moss, and when bare so jagged as to wound one's hands fearfully – and the Gusts came so very sudden and strong, that the going up was slow, and difficult and earnest – and the coming down, not only all that, but likewise extremely dangerous. However, I have always found this *stretched and anxious* state of mind favourable to depth of pleasurable Impression, in the resting Places and *lownding* Coves.

The motives that took Coleridge to high, steep places were much the same as those that activate most rock-climbers to this day: the physical thrill of it; the dramatic scenery all round; the 'stretched and anxious state of mind' that sharpens one's feelings and perceptions – the increased 'Intensity of the Feeling of Life' which always came to him, he said, when he went into the hills. It is almost tempting to believe that, had Coleridge stayed in the Lake District, the sport of rock-climbing might have emerged some 80 years before it did. It is not very likely, though. Not long after he completed his 'circumcursion' his health declined and his opium consumption increased. He was, anyway, a solitary scrambler, preferring to adventure alone. And it is doubtful whether he would have found anyone willing to accompany him.

He dropped down the steep path to Cam Spout, admiring the many waterfalls on the way:

> When I had almost reached the bottom of the Hill, I stood so as to command the whole 8 Waterfalls, with the great triangle-Crag looking in above them, and on the one side of them the enormous and more than perpendicular Precipices and *Bull's-Brows* of Sca'Fell!

The 'Bull's-Brows' would be the dark and imposing cliffs of Scafell's East Buttress, a popular playground for modern climbers.

At the foot of the slope, the ground levels out into a

wide hanging valley, with a superb cirque of craggy ridges and mountain tops all round. Just below, the infant River Esk begins its journey to the Irish Sea. Coleridge swung to the right here, keeping above the river and passing beneath the crags of Cam Spout. The thunderstorm was now very close upon him:

> Just at the bottom of the Hill I saw on before me in the Vale, lying just above the River on the side of a Hill, one, two, three, four Objects, I could not distinguish whether Peat-hovels, or hovel-shaped Stones – I thought in my mind that 3 of them would turn out to be stones – but that the fourth was certainly a Hovel. I went on toward them, crossing and recrossing the Becks and the River and found that they were all huge Stones – the one nearest the Beck which I had determined to be really a Hovel, retained its likeness when I was close beside – in size it is nearly equal to the famous Bowder Stone, but in every other respect greatly superior to it – it has a complete Roof, and that perfectly *thatched* with weeds, and Heath and Mountain-Ash Bushes. . . .

This group of half a dozen large boulders is now called Sampson's Stones. They are quite impressive – one of them, as Coleridge said, is completely roofed with vegetation – but none of them can justly be likened to Borrowdale's famous Bowder Stone, either for size or for the remarkable way it is poised on a knife-edge.

I descended from the summit of Scafell by way of the very steep and heavily eroded path to Foxes Tarn. Despite its name, it is no more than a small and gloomy pond, getting smaller all the time as rubble and rocks drop into it from above. Since I passed by, I am told, a National Trust team has been up there, clearing some of the stones from the tarn and building a rock wall to protect it from further incursions. Below the tarn, a slithery scramble down a gully leads to the main path from the Mickledore Gap. Here I rejoined Coleridge's route and began to descend, as he had done, towards Eskdale, admiring the superb waterfalls and the wild, widening view ahead.

Coleridge surveyed the scene, then pushed on:

> ... and came to a little Village of Sheep-folds – there
> were 5 together – and the redding Stuff, and the Shears,
> and an old Pot, was in the Passage of the first of them.
> Here I found an imperfect shelter from a Thunder-
> shower – accompanied with such Echoes! O God!
> what thoughts were mine! O how I wished for Health
> and Strength that I might wander about for a Month
> together, in the stormiest month of the year, among
> these Places, so lonely and savage and full of sounds!

It is a cry from the heart and one that was not answered – the
health and strength were not granted him in the months and
years to come.

The huddle of sheep enclosures he described is still there,
though it has now fallen into ruins. Coleridge sheltered till the
storm passed:

> After the Thunder-storm I shouted out all your names
> in the Sheep-fold – when Echo came upon Echo – and
> then Hartley and Derwent and then I laughed and
> shouted Joanna – It leaves all the Echoes I ever heard
> far far behind, in number, distinctness, and *humanness*
> of Voice – and then not to forget an old Friend I made
> them all say Dr. Dodd etc. –

This was Dr William Dodd, previously chaplain to the King and
the first anthologiser of Shakespeare (*The Beauties of Shakespeare* was published in 1752), who had become nationally
famous when found guilty of forging a bond for £4,200. Dr
Johnson was prominent among those who worked to get his
reprieve from the death sentence, but in vain – Dr Dodd was
executed in 1777. It is not clear why his name should have
sprung into Coleridge's mind at this juncture. The other names,
though, are easily explained. Hartley and Derwent were his
young sons. Joanna was Sara Hutchinson's younger sister.

There is some mystery about these echoes that Coleridge
sent reverberating around the crags. I tried shouting from the

same point and the response I got was only just audible. Some time later I returned with two friends and we all shouted as loudly as we could, separately and then together, and the results fell far short of Coleridge's description. How can an echo effect have disappeared in two centuries?

It is not clear which route Coleridge followed on his descent into Eskdale; the names he gives in his letter – 'Maddock How' and 'Scale Gill Force' – do not appear on modern maps. He talks, however, of seeing more fine waterfalls, so I opted to follow the line of the river. At one point, where it runs through a steep-sided and heavily vegetated rocky gorge, I had to make a wide detour. It is a beautiful stretch of water, sometimes plunging wildly down in a foaming fury of white spray, at other times forming deep pools of startling turquoise clarity.

In his letter Coleridge remarked on the continuous water sounds and wondered if the word 'Scale' (common among Lakeland placenames) derived from *scalle* which, he said, signified 'a deafening Noise'. Etymology was not a science in 1802, and Coleridge inclined to the romantic, onomatopaeic approach. Soon after he arrived in Keswick, for example, he wrote to a friend surmising that the river below his house, the Greta, might have got its name from the old meaning of the word *greet*, 'to weep and wail and roar in grief'. Modern scholarship says *scale*, in its Cumbrian usage, comes from the Old Norse word *skali*, which referred to the sort of rough, temporary shed often found by the high summer pastures of Norway. The close connection between the placenames and dialect words of the Lake District region and the Old Norse language was first pointed out, in 1819, by Thomas De Quincey in an article published in the *Westmorland Gazette* – he was the paper's editor at the time – entitled 'The Danish Origin of the Lake Country Dialect'.

At the foot of Esk Falls the path crosses Lingcove Bridge, then swings to the right, following the river. A little further on, passing beneath Heron Crag, I saw two climbers enjoying the steep rock in the late afternoon sun. In his letter, Coleridge goes on:

... Well, I passed thro' some sweet pretty Fields, and
came to a large Farm-house where I am now writing –
The place is called Toes or *Te* as – the master's name
John Vicars Towers – they received me hospitably – I
drank Tea here and they begged me to pass the Night –
which I did and supped of some excellent Salmonlings,
which Towers had brought from Ravenglass whither
he had been, as holding under the Earl of Egremont,
and obliged 'to ride the Fair' – a custom introduced
during the times of Insecurity and piratical Incursion
for the Protection of Ravenglass Fair.

William Hutchinson refers to this ancient custom whereby
tenants of the Earl had to attend Ravenglass Fair for three days
each year 'to defend the merchandise against free-booters, and
a foreign enemy; such was the wretched state of this country in
former times, that all such protection was scarce sufficient'.

The farm where Coleridge stayed that night is now known
as Taw House Farm. For the past 50 years and more, Mr George
Ellwood has lived there with his wife, renting the place from
the National Trust, looking after many Herdwick sheep and
some cattle with the help of his son Ian and several lively dogs.
They take bed and breakfast guests but were full up when I
arrived, so I had to walk on another mile or so and get a room
at the Woolpack Inn.

Taw House Farm looks much as it must have done when
Coleridge lodged there. It was a new building then: a datestone
over the front door says 'John and Betty 1789'. It is rather worn
and weathered now and there is one indication of late-twentieth-
century life – a Sky Television satellite dish plugged to the front
wall.

That evening, Coleridge would almost certainly have told
John Vicars Towers about his adventure on Scafell. A few years
later, according to local legend, Towers and Thomas Tyson of
Wasdale Head met at the Mickledore Gap and together made
the first ascent of the Broad Stand route.

CHAPTER EIGHT

The Lakeless Valleys

My evening at the Woolpack proved eventful. I had a bath and went down to the bar to find it already lively with holiday visitors and locals. Within moments, a large man approached and asked if I was Alan Hankinson. He recognised me from a television film I had made about Lake District rock-climbing. His name was Ian Finlinson. He and his family – from Holcombe, near Bath – were on a fell-walking holiday and in a state of some elation since, the day before, he and his son Andrew had successfully completed a marathon walk known as the Woolpack Round.

This punishing form of endurance test has been popular, among the fit and masochistic, for well over 100 years. Several valleys offer their own 'big challenge' to dedicated or competitive walkers. They begin and end at the same point and take the form of a long circular or horseshoe-shaped walk along the high summits, which has to be completed in a stated time. The one at Wasdale head is called the Mosedale Horseshoe. Perhaps the most famous is the Bob Graham Round, named in honour of a man who ran a guesthouse in Keswick. In June 1932, he set off from the Moot Hall in the centre of the town and within the next 24 hours gained 42 summits, covering 72 miles, ascending and descending some 27,000 feet – not far short of the height of Mount Everest. Bob Graham did it with 21 minutes to spare and his record stood for the next 28 years, though it has been broken many times since then.

It was not until the late 1960s that a marathon challenge was devised for Eskdale by three regulars at the Woolpack. The 'Round' starts and finishes at the inn. To qualify, the walker has to touch all the summits that encircle the valley head – Harter Fell, Hardknott Pass, Crinkle Crags, Bow Fell, Esk Pike, Scafell Pike, Scafell and Slight Side. He or she can do it either clockwise or anti-clockwise. Men have to complete the route in under 11 hours – women within 12. The distance is $18\frac{3}{4}$ miles, involving more than 6,700 feet of up and down, most of it on rough ground. The reward, which does not seem over-generous, is a free pint – of beer or some soft drink – when you get back.

They keep a book behind the bar for people to record their achievements and many have done 'the Round' in the past 30 years, most of them within the time limits. Many fought their way through atrocious weather. Some, to be different, did it in the dark. Some have worked out longer and more desperate variations. One of the founders, Gerry Turner of Goole in North Humberside, did it 13 times in 11 years, and signed off his final account with the words, 'I bow out before I pass out.' Many of the fastest times have been recorded, not surprisingly, by instructors from the Outward Bound Mountaineering School further down the valley. Two of them hold the current record, an amazing three hours five minutes. As yet, the youngest person to do it is Andrew Finlinson, who was ten years old on 16th August 1989 when he arrived back at the inn with six minutes to spare and claimed his pint of Coke. His father, who had accompanied him, said they had been in cloud and rain most of the way. They were very tired on the final stretch, but proud and delighted to have done it.

As a mountain walker, Coleridge had both speed and stamina, but I doubt whether he would have been interested by this sort of thing. For him, fell-walking was more about freedom than competitiveness.

He spent the first part of the sixth morning of his walk writing the vivid account of his descent from Scafell the previous day. He was impressed by his hosts and ventured some further flights of imaginative etymology:

> They were a fine Family – and a Girl who did not look more than 12 years old, but was nearly 15, was very beautiful – with hair like vine-tendrils. She had been long ill – and was a sickly child –'Ah poor Bairn! (said the Mother) worse luck for her – she looks like a Quality Bairn, as you may say'. This man's Ancestors have been time out of mind in the Vale, and here I

found that the common Names, Towers and Tozers, are the same – *er* signifies 'upon' – as Mite-er-dale the Dale upon the River Mite – Donnerdale, a contraction of Duddon-er-dale, the Dale upon the River Duddon – So Towers, pronounced in the Vale *Te-ars*, and Tozers are those who live on *the Toes*, i.e. upon the *Knobbly* feet of the Mountain.

After breakfast he and John Vicars Towers went out to look round the valley head, the region which, had the Forestry Commission won the battle of the 1930s, would now be blanketed in conifers.

Coleridge had studied Hutchinson's *History of the County of Cumberland,* published eight years before, and remembered the passage which read: 'On a stone near Buck-Cragg, are the impressions of the foot of a man, a boy, and a dog, without any marks of tooling, or instrument'. I imagine he asked Towers to show him the stone:

I passed on, a little way, till I came under a huge Crag, called Buck Crag – and immediately under this is four-foot Stone – having on it the clear marks of four foot-steps. The Stone is in its whole breadth just 36 inches (I measured it exactly) but the part that contains the marks is raised above the other part, and is just $20\frac{1}{2}$ Inches. The length of the Stone is $32\frac{1}{2}$ Inches. The first foot-mark is an Ox's foot – nothing can be conceived more exact – this is $5\frac{3}{4}$ Inches wide – the second is a Boy's shoe in the Snow, $9\frac{1}{2}$ Inches in length – this too is the very Thing itself, the Heel, the bend of the Foot etc. – the third is the Foot-step to the very Life of a Mastiff Dog – and the fourth is *Derwent's very own first little Shoe,* 4 Inches in length and O! it is the sweetest Baby shoe that ever was seen ... this really does work upon my imagination very powerfully, and I will try to construct a Tale upon it – the place too is so very, very wild. I delighted the Shepherd by my admiration, and the four foot Stone is my own

> Christening, and Towers undertakes it shall hereafter
> go by that name for hitherto it has been nameless.

The name has survived; the people at the farm still know it as 'the four-foot stone'.

I was unable to find it, following Coleridge's directions. His 'Buck Crag' does not appear on modern maps so I searched about at the foot of Brock Crag – as the closest aural equivalent – but, although there are hundreds of stones in the area, none of them matched the description. I returned to Taw House Farm and Ian Ellwood gave me detailed directions. I went higher this time, to the ground above Brock Crag, and again failed. I returned to Eskdale months later, as I was nearing this section of the book, and got Ian to walk up with me and show me where it is.

It was not surprising that I had failed to find it or, indeed, that some people in recent years have said that the stone has disappeared altogether. It is a singularly undistinguished lump of dark rock, lying on the path below High Scarth Crag. Once it is pointed out, however, there is no doubt that this is it. Its dimensions are exactly as Coleridge described; he used notches on his besom-stick to get the measurements exact. His description of the markings is clear and precise. Even so it is a small piece of stone, lying low on the ground, and very easily missed. Thousands walk by every year without noticing it. Although the four indentations do resemble various footmarks, it is hard to see why Coleridge found it so fascinating. To me at any rate, it is no more than a rather odd coincidence that a stone should have become pitted in this way by natural wear and tear. To Coleridge, it was clearly remarkable and highly suggestive, though his plan to build a story around it, like so many of his schemes, came to nothing.

It seems even odder that Coleridge should have given so much attention to this stone, and yet made no attempt to inspect the remains of the Roman fort near the foot of Hardknott Pass. He walked just below the plateau where the fort was built. And he must have known about it because Hutchinson devotes a full page, with a diagram, to describing the place which, he says, 'has evidently been intended as a fortress, for the defence of that pass over the mountains'. According to Hutchinson, two men, inspecting the foundations of some of the fort's inner buildings in the year 1792, 'met with a great many fragments of brick, apparently Roman'. But, as was the case with old church buildings and monastic ruins, these Roman remains failed to arouse Coleridge's curiosity.

The fort was thoroughly excavated about a century after Coleridge passed by. It was a sizeable building with barracks, a granary, the obligatory Roman bath-houses and a parade ground, designed to accommodate some 500 infantrymen. Scholars believe it was built at the beginning of the second century AD – one of a chain of forts between the port of Ravenglass and Hadrian's Wall – and abandoned, for unknown reasons, towards the end of that century. All that can be seen now are the remains of the stone walls, but they give an impression of what the fort must have been like when it was in use; and the position is superb, commanding wide views down Eskdale Valley to the coast and across the valley head to the Scafells. It is a popular spot for those motor-borne tourists who are prepared to tackle the narrow, steep and twisting roads over Wrynose and Hardknott passes. Many of them pause to consider the culture and climate shock sustained by soldiers who found themselves posted to this remote and windswept mountainside. It is known that the fort was garrisoned at one time by men from the Adriatic coast of what is now Yugoslavia.

When he got back to the farmhouse about midday, Coleridge immediately sat down to recount the morning's excursion for Sara Hutchinson. He concluded:

> ... And so I returned and have found a Pedlar here of
> an interesting Physiognomy – and here I must leave
> off – for Dinner is ready –

That abrupt termination marks the end of his second Scafell letter, or the point at which Sara chose to halt her transcription. He had every intention of completing his account of the 'circumcursion', but never got round to it. There was a pile of correspondence waiting to be dealt with when he arrived home. Then his oldest and most loyal friend, Charles Lamb, together with his sister Mary, arrived to stay three weeks at Greta Hall. Soon after that, Coleridge's domestic troubles closed in on him once more.

The fact that he never finished what he called 'the Great-sheet Letter' means that the last three and a half days of his walk are not so fully documented as the first part of the journey. It is possible, however, to establish the route he followed, more or less, and to learn something of his thoughts and feelings. He still wrote assiduously in the *Notebook* as he went along, and as soon as he got home he summarised his walk in letters to Sara and to Robert Southey.

As Coleridge had done, I spent most of the morning of the sixth day exploring the valley head, trying to work out exactly where he had been (without much success), and failing to find the 'four-foot stone'. I visited Taw House Farm and learned that I was not the first person to turn up there, following the 'circumcursion' trail. Apparently, a man called Mr Mulvaney, who came from somewhere in Surrey, had called on the Ellwoods in the early 1970s and told them he was retracing the route with a view to writing something about it. As far as they knew, though, nothing had been published. Mr Mulvaney's last visit had been in 1973. Two or three years ago they heard that he had died.

Coleridge had a midday meal at the farm, then set off, about 1.30 p.m., on the next stage of the walk, heading west-wards down the Eskdale valley. From time to time he stopped to make notes about the configuration of the landscape, the names of the hills and his impressions:

> ... but never sure were lovelyer human Dwellings than these nested in Trees at the foot of the Fells, and in among the intervening Hills. After you have left Sca'Fell and his Progeny behind you, the Fells on each side are low, rough and ragged with Bushwood.

His plan was to cross over the ridge of low hills that separate Eskdale from Dunnerdale, the valley of the River Duddon. He passed through the little village of Boot and close by the Church of St Catherine, first built in the twelfth century and rebuilt in the nineteenth. It stands in a lovely secluded riverside situation. Coleridge, true to his custom, walked on, but I paused here to look for the graves of the two men who had been his hosts on the previous nights. John Vicars Towers died in 1817 at the age of 71. Close to his grave is that of his friend Thomas Tyson, 'Wasdale Head Yeoman' as it says on the headstone, who died in 1842, aged 82. Thomas's parents are also buried here, and their headstone is incised with the words:

> All you, my friends, wipe off your tears,
> Here I must lie till Christ appears,
> And when he comes I hope to rise
> Unto a life that never dies.

It reminded me of the 'Epitaph' Coleridge wrote for himself in the last winter of his life, 1833–4, in the house of Dr and Mrs Gillman at the top of Highgate Hill, overlooking London, where he had been carefully looked after for the last 18 years of his life:

> Stop, Christian passer-by! – Stop, child of God,
> And read with gentle breast. Beneath this sod
> A poet lies, or that which once seem'd he.
> O, lift one thought in prayer for S.T.C.;
> That he who many a year with toil of breath
> Found death in life, may here find life in death!
> Mercy for praise – to be forgiven for fame
> He ask'd, and hoped, through Christ. Do thou the same!

Below the church there is a delightful stretch of river with deep green pools and pale grey rocks. A few minutes' walk takes you off the road and clear of all traffic sounds into a world of sylvan beauty. Yet all the visiting motorists, when I passed by, had elected to set up their camping chairs and tables to picnic alongside their parked cars.

A little further along I heard a sudden, loud whistling sound behind me and turned to see the miniature railway engine, generally known as 'La'al Ratty', heading back to Ravenglass. (The full and proper title of the line is 'The Ravenglass and Eskdale Railway'.) A narrow-gauge line was constructed up the

Eskdale valley in the 1870s, chiefly to carry iron ore down to the main coastal railway line, though it was soon taking passengers as well. This venture closed down in 1908, but a new company was formed a few years later, primarily to ferry granite from the quarry at Beckfoot. This, too, had foundered by 1960, and it looked as if that was the end of any Eskdale railway. But the love of steam traction is a powerful passion in Britain, and before long the Ravenglass and Eskdale Railway Preservation Society was in action. Ever since, with increasing success, their small but perfectly formed and brightly shining locomotives have towed carriageloads of tourists up and down the 7 miles of track. It is billed as 'the most beautiful train journey in England'. Strictly speaking, I suppose, a railway train puffing its way up towards the heart of the mountains amounts to an 'alien intrusion', in Wordsworth's phrase, but for most people it makes a slightly whimsical and cheering sight.

In his *Notebook* Coleridge says he should have crossed the River Esk at Dalegarth Hall and turned southwards at that point, but instead he went 2 miles further on before changing direction. So I walked on, too, crossed the river at Forge Bridge, and found a path that promised a route over Brantrake Crags and Brantrake Moss and so to Devoke Water.

A sign indicated a bridle path and for a while it was a wide grassy track running alongside a dry-stone wall. Then it swung suddenly and steeply uphill and the path disappeared under a dense covering of bracken. 'It's been a long time,' I muttered angrily, as I fought my way through this treacherous jungle, 'since anyone got a horse up here.'

Coleridge went over by way of what he calls 'Easterfield Common' which appears on none of today's maps. Judging from his account, however, he must have ascended somewhere in this region, though he makes no mention of having to struggle through waist-high bracken.

There is much more of this noxious growth on the Lake District hillsides today than there was 200 years ago. The farms were smaller then and every square foot of land had to be worked. Labour was far cheaper and more plentiful, and the hired men either burnt the bracken back or scythed it down to make winter bedding for the cattle. There were more cattle, too, on the lower slopes, and they were prepared to eat young bracken shoots and happy to trample it down at any time.

For over a century the small farms have been disappearing, the labour force diminishing. Cattle are now grazed in the valley fields. As a result, the bracken has spread across the fellsides, up to the 1,000-foot contour line. It is a persistent coloniser, it is not easily discouraged, and the sheep will not eat it. No weed-killer has been devised that can destroy it. It eliminates all other forms of vegetation and repels most forms of wildlife, except for flies and black beetles. It exudes a nasty smell in the summer, and some scientists have accused it of being cancer-causing.

Except from the scenic point of view – especially in the autumn when it casts a golden splendour across many hillsides – there is nothing to be said for bracken. From the fell-walker's point of view, there is much to be said against it. The man who devises a way of making it both nutritious and appetising to sheep will win the gratitude of millions.

I finally clawed my way clear and emerged on to open, boggy moorland, with cotton grass and many lovely and complex mosses, all shades of green and grey. Ahead was the tarn called Devoke Water. I stopped to look round. To the north-east, Scafell Pike and its giant neighbours were clear of cloud. To the north-west, I could make out the steaming towers of Sellafield. The sight reminded me that the regions I was crossing, Eskdale and Dunnerdale, were among those worst affected in April 1986 when radioactive rain fell on the mountains of North Wales and the Lake District from a cloud that had come thousands of miles, from the explosion and fire at Chernobyl in Byelorussia. More than four years on, there are still 'hot spots' in these hills, and the farmers have to have their sheep checked with geiger-counters before they are allowed to move them.

There was no one else about. I heard a lamb bleating for its lost mother. A hawk of some kind moved slowly overhead, emitting a loud, sad, keening cry. There was a light, warm breeze and the sun shone. It was hard to think of this as poisoned land. For the first time on the whole trip I was able to take off my anorak, stuff it into the rucksack, and stroll down to the water's edge in shirtsleeves.

Coleridge paused here to make a few notes:

> Descended on the other side of Easterfield Common, crossed a moss, and ascended another and came out upon Devoke, a good large Tairn with naked Banks, and a tiny Island covered with Sea fowl, two of which, and afterwards four, flew round about above me, wailing and [? barking/baiting], then dipped down low, and made a dead *dart* along over my head, so that I could hear the clang of the wings, and altering its Note to a noise of anger and menace.

There were no angry seabirds in evidence when I was there. Coleridge speaks of a boat-house on the shore and it is still there. Nearby two couples were pitching their tents. There was a sign indicating that the fishing here was the preserve of Millom Angling Association.

Coleridge spent some time looking about for 'the ruins of the city of Barnscar', which he had read about in Hutchinson who said that local tradition claimed that the Danes had established a sizeable settlement here. Coleridge noted:

> ... I found nothing, after most patient search, that I could distinguish from any part of the Fell.

I know the feeling. More than once I have been impressed by the anthropologist's 'eye of faith' when confronting some scarcely perceptible bulge or depression in the ground. But on this occasion Coleridge was simply looking in the wrong place. What is left of the Barnscar settlement is more than a mile to the west of Devoke Water.

In the late afternoon he dropped down to Ulpha Kirk by the River Duddon. The two valleys he visited this day, Eskdale and Dunnerdale, are alike in one important respect; neither of them has a lake. In most other ways, they are entirely different. Eskdale is very grand at the head of the valley; and lower down, the Esk runs through a green and pleasant and varied and open vale. There is a feeling of expansiveness about it. The Duddon, on the other hand, plunges down towards the sea along a narrow, steep-sided valley. The river is dominant. The vale is enclosed and private and also luxuriant; grasses and ferns and plants, shrubs and trees, all seem to thrive and flourish here with more than usual vigour.

Coleridge was enraptured. His *Notebook* jottings are full of his excitement: '... a most romantic vale ... eminently picturesque ... O lovely lovely Vale!'

Cumbria's two great poets have followed the river from its source on Wrynose Fell to the Irish Sea. Wordsworth wrote a sequence of 34 sonnets, describing the journey. And more than a century later Norman Nicholson paid a shorter but no less powerful tribute 'To the River Duddon', which he began by recalling his predecessor:

> I wonder, Duddon, if you still remember
> An oldish man with a nose like a pony's nose,
> Broad bones, legs long and lean but strong enough
> To carry him over Hard Knott at 70 years of age ....

CHAPTER NINE

The Southern Lakes

The next morning Coleridge walked a little way down the river, then turned off the road and scrambled up a steep, rocky slope to the top of a small hill:

> Here it was seated on this Mount, on Saturday, August 7, that I resolved to write under the name The Soother of Absence, the topographical poem which I had long mummel'd about in my mind, and the day before thought of under the name of the Bards of Helvellin or the Stone Hovels.

Clearly, he had been thinking for some time of writing a poem based on his extensive wanderings about the fells and his responses to the experience. I imagine it would probably have been a philosophical/narrative poem in the Wordsworthian manner, possibly expressing the theme he had outlined in a letter to his brother George more than four years before:

> I love fields and woods and mountains with almost a visionary fondness – and because I have found benevolence and quietness growing within me as that fondness has increased, therefore I should wish to be the means of implanting it in others – and to destroy the bad passions not by combating them, but by keeping them in inaction.

The projected poem was never written. As he knew better than anyone and regretted more deeply than anything else, the power of true poetry had already left him. For all the teeming images and ideas that crowd the pages of his letters and *Notebooks*, he could no longer work – transmute – them into poetry. His 'shaping Spirit of the Imagination' had lost its power. He tried to revive it when he got back to Greta Hall at the end of the 'circumcursion', but the results were disappointing. The most sustained attempt led to a blank verse narrative poem called 'The Picture', which was published in the *Morning Post* in early September 1802. It opened with these lines:

> Through weeds and thorns, and matted underwood
> I force my way; now climb, and now descend
> O'er rocks, or bare or mossy, with wild foot
> Crushing the purple whorts: while oft unseen,
> Hurrying along the drifted forest leaves,
> The scared snake rustles. Onwards still I toil,
> I know not, ask not whither! A new joy,
> Lovely as light, sudden as summer gust,
> And gladsome as the first-born of the spring,
> Beckons me on, or follows from behind,
> Playmate, or guide! The master-passion quelled,
> I feel that I am free.

The 'master-passion' is love for a woman – he must have been thinking of Sara Hutchinson and his efforts to escape from his love for her. The poem resumes:

> Here Wisdom might resort, and here Remorse;
> Here too the love-lorn man, who, sick in soul,
> And of this busy human heart aweary,
> Worships the spirit of unconscious life
> In tree or wild flower. – Gentle lunatic!
> If so he might not wholly cease to be,
> He would far rather not be that he is:
> But would be something that he knows not of,
> In winds or waters, or among the rocks!

Many of the fundamental Coleridgean themes are there, but by this time it was Wordsworth not Coleridge who could state them with full poetic force.

There is one further passage that seems to derive from his fell-walking. It occurs in a poem, published in the *Morning Post* in mid-September 1802, which he called 'Hymn before Sun-rise in the Vale of Chamouni'. He had never been to Chamonix, never seen the snow slopes and crags and glaciers of Mont Blanc. He got his images, clearly, from much nearer home:

And you, ye five wild torrents fiercely glad!
Who called you forth from night and utter death,
From dark and icy caverns called you forth,
Down those precipitous, black, jagged rocks,
For ever shattered and the same for ever?
Who gave you your invulnerable life,
Your strength, your speed, your fury, and your joy,
Unceasing thunder and eternal foam?

The poem is a hymn of praise to God the creator who, as everyone knows, rested on the seventh day. Coleridge did not. He walked over Dunnerdale Fells to Broughton Mills, the southernmost point of his tour, then turned north for Coniston, heading home. For the first and last time on the whole trip, he got lost.

Dunnerdale Fells are low by Lake District standards and little-visited even today. They offer a wilderness of small crags and grassy slopes and deep bracken, full of streams and ponds known as 'dubs' in these parts. There are no prominent features to guide you and it is not surprising that Coleridge, without a compass, should have missed his way:

> I climb over the Fell, taking to my left a little, wind around (under and between) low crags, and come to two Dubs in the shape of an 8.... It must have been here that I lost my way, for I now went on till I found myself coming down upon Ulpha again, about a mile above the House and Kirk which I had just quitted – however I was not sorry to have another view of that lovely Place ... I saw Houses to my right, and an old Man with his Daughter, a sweet Girl, burning Bracken – went up to him and talked with him and the lovely Girl in the midst of the Huge Volumes of Smoke, and found I had gone two miles wrong – which yet I could scarcely believe....

The old man redirected him and he made his way, successfully this time, over to the quiet hamlet of Broughton Mills. The fells here are low and undramatic compared to those further north, but full of interest and surprises. I set off uphill, passing the school, and followed a lovely grassy track through the woods, to emerge on to open fell. It was a fresh morning and there was the noise of running water all round. Higher up there were broad views to the south, the sands of the Duddon estuary and the rolling green hills of North Lancashire.

There is an old pub at Broughton Mills, the Blacksmith's Arms, built in 1748, and it was here that Coleridge refreshed himself:

> Dined on Oatcake and Cheese, with a pint of Ale, and 2 glasses of Rum and water sweetened with preserved Gooseberries at the Ale house – Cassons' – the son, William Casson, got a pleurisy and abcess in his side by overheating himself and then starving himself in breaking up the Ice for the Mill – but being a Scholar, he gets his cloathes and a little money besides by teaching a lile lock of Bairns – his Father and Mother that keep the Public House, give him his meat. ['Starving' is used in the North Country sense – 'getting very cold'.]

I sat outside, writing up my notes, until noon when the pub opened. The interior looked as if it had hardly been touched, apart from an occasional dusting, since Coleridge was there. So far, it seemed, the Blacksmith's Arms had happily resisted the modern brewers' mania for turning everything to gilt and plush and formica. The bar was small and dark and snug, a place of oak panelling and massive black beams and well-worn wooden benches at ancient wooden tables. The atmosphere was relaxed and friendly, completely unpretentious. The beer was good and the barmaid charming.

We chatted about fell-walking and rock-climbing, both of which she enjoyed, and Broughton's agricultural show which was on soon. When I heard that she drove over each day from her home in Millom, I asked if she had known Norman Nicholson. 'Everyone in Millom knew him,' she said. 'He used to come to school and read his poems to us. A marvellous man.'

From Broughton Mills, Coleridge turned northwards. It is

about 4 miles to Torver, and he took a quiet country lane that gave fine views across the valley to wooded, rocky hills with bigger mountain ridges behind them. He was moved to reflect upon the almost impossible task confronting the painter who attempts this type of landscape:

> N.B. – one effect of the magnitude of surrounding objects – it gives to shapes a narrowness of width, exceedingly favourable to boldness, an approximating to a sharp point, which being comparative loses its effect upon paper – because you can scarcely give the real shape, preserving its true relative dimensions, besides in a picture you can only take a part of the view; but in nature, the whole, perhaps 20 fold more than you draw, appears to you, each part modified by all the rest ...

It was, he says, 'a day of sun and Clouds, with a thousand Shadows on the Hills'. Further on, from a small hilltop, he looked to his right and behind him to see the wide valley spreading towards the sea. When I walked that lane, in similar weather, the fields and hedgerows were alive with birds – swifts and swallows, chaffinches and magpies and hedge-sparrows. There were abundant and succulent blackberries too. It is a metalled road but narrow, and for well over an hour I cruised along in the sunshine without seeing a car or a single other person. You descend to the main road just before Torver, however, so the last 3 miles of the walk to Coniston are altogether different.

I made the final part of the walk much more pleasant and interesting by turning right, beyond Torver, on to the path that leads to the shores of Coniston Water. The Planning Board has installed new gates and stiles and clear signs to ensure that no one misses the way. It is a delightful path through quiet woodland and I still seemed to have the whole region to myself, so it came as a considerable surprise to emerge from the trees, on to the lakeshore, and be confronted with a scene of great animation and colour. There were bright tents in the meadows, and the lake itself was alive with the multicoloured sails of scores of fast-moving craft – yachts and catamarans and, outnumbering them all, swarms of windsurfers, fighting to hold course in the blusterous south-westerly wind, making that marvellous ripping sound that comes when the board is moving fast.

On the opposite side of the lake, glistening white in the sunshine, I could see the jumbled outlines of Brantwood, the home of John Ruskin for the last 28 years of his life. This is another area of the Lake District, like the Newlands Valley, that is uncommonly rich in literary association. Here, though, it is almost as if there were a dynasty of distinguished names.

Ruskin bought Brantwood in 1871 from a man called William Linton, whose wife Lynn was a very popular novelist of the period. Ruskin was then at the height of his fame and powers and for a few years he was able to enjoy his lakeside home to the full, but then that powerful mind suffered a total collapse. The incomparably eloquent voice was silenced and he was sometimes quite mad; but the terrible final years were made more bearable by the help and company of his secretary, William Gershom Collingwood.

Collingwood was a man of multifarious accomplishments – a talented artist, a musician and a novelist; a devoted family man; immensely learned about all aspects of Lake District history; an all-rounder in the Renaissance manner, keen on small-boat sailing and swimming, fell-walking and rock-climbing. By all accounts, he was also a generous-spirited man, always ready to help young people, and among those he befriended in the early years of this century was an aspiring poet called Arthur Ransome. Ransome is read and remembered today chiefly as the author of *Swallows and Amazons* and many other adventure stories for children set on and around the lakes of Coniston and Windermere. But he was a fascinating man in many ways, a great sailor and fisherman whose work as a foreign correspondent led to remarkable adventures. He was in St Petersburg in October 1917, played chess with Lenin, fell in love with Trotsky's secretary (whom he later married), and was almost executed as a spy when the revolutionaries were fighting the White Russian forces.

Nonetheless, it is the spirit of Ruskin, though he died in

1900, that still presides over the Coniston area. His grave is in Coniston churchyard; and 100 yards away, the town's old-fashioned museum is crammed with his drawings, sketchbooks, pictures and letters, as well as his collections of minerals and fossils. Most impressive of all, there is Brantwood itself. In the 1930s the house was set up as a sort of national memorial to the great prophetic figure. For many years it was a dark and depressing place, almost as if the ghost of the demented old man still haunted it. Now it has been happily transformed into an airy and elegant house, full of fascinating things, properly representing Ruskin in his prime.

Many people, I imagine, if they were asked to choose the half-dozen most seminal thinkers in England in the nineteenth century, would name both Ruskin and Coleridge. They had some qualities in common – powerful and original minds, and the ability to express their thoughts with vivid fluency. They both loved mountains, too, but in very different ways. Ruskin's interest was aesthetic and spiritual; Coleridge's was athletic as well. The best views, Ruskin said, were those from the valleys. He poured invective on the mountaineers who competed to make first ascents and then made quiet Alpine villages resound with their celebrations. There was a basic difference, too, in the way they approached great problems. Coleridge's way was to think, deeply, and expound his ideas. Ruskin did that, but he also believed in action. A passionate social reformer, he was for ever setting up groups to try to improve the quality of the national life and counteract the effects of the corrupting factory system. He poured money into his causes. That was yet another difference between them. Ruskin always had plenty of money. Coleridge never had enough.

When Coleridge passed that way, Brantwood was a modest cottage in the woods, only five years old. He did not even notice it as he surveyed the area and tried to pinpoint its distinguishing qualities in his *Notebook*:

> Coniston Lake is a fine mixture of the aweful and the pleasing Simple – of one-colored dark Rocks, and pastoral Hills below.

Coniston is doubtless a worthy Compeer of the Stateliest, an equal Coheir of Nature with Keswick, Wyndermere, and Ulswater. Its distinguishing character I think is its perfect and easy comprehensibility. At its foot the Hills are low, but of a various out-line – from the Foot to within a mile of the Head, the Hills on either side are of no great permanent Interest, tho' susceptible no doubt of a very high one from the accidents of Nature, that must be so frequent here, of broken Sunlights, Clouds and Storm. The Head of the Lake is an admirable junction of awful and of pleasing Simplicity. It is beyond all the other lakes perfectly intelligible ... – at the head of the Lake ... high mountains of a remarkable sternness and simplicity, one-colored, as seen at a distance, and dark-colored – its boldest parts are first, the Bell and the Scrow, two black Peaks, perfectly breast-shaped and lying abreast of each other, the whole Bosom of a Brobdignag Negress....

The Bell and the Scrow (which is called Foul Scrow on modern maps) are small but steep-sided hills on your left as you leave Coniston by the Coppermines Valley track. I walked all round them but failed to find the angle of view that gave Coleridge the impression of the breast of some giant negress.

He spent the night at the Black Bull Hotel in the centre of Coniston, which claims to date from the sixteenth century. I managed to get a room there too, the only time on the whole trip when I was able to sleep under the same roof as he did. The bar has an air of some antiquity, with black beams and glistening pewter on the walls and a stone fireplace. I found it very crowded, with a constant queue at the bar and waiters rushing in and out with plateloads of food. It was a warm evening and many people were sitting at the tables outside. Three teenage buskers – a girl violinist, a male guitarist, and another girl to turn the music over and go round collecting money – were doing a good trade.

The next morning Coleridge surveyed the northern end of

the lake, which he found much more domesticated than the country he had been travelling through so far:

> The Houses, Gardens, fields and woodland upon this crescent Hill are all in admirable *keeping*, various as heart can wish, yet all sweet Brothers and Sisters – so various that when together you see small likeness – so like that when separate, you might mistake one for the other ....
>
> ... observe from Torver thro' Coniston the force of imitation in the Gardens and sweet Porches, and everywhere clipped yews, in obelisks and fine arches....

Coniston had long prospered from copper-mining and slate-quarrying, and by the start of the nineteenth century the whole of this region of the southern lakes, Coniston and Windermere, was beginning to attract wealthy people from well outside the Lake District who wanted holiday or retirement homes in rural surroundings. It was happening around the shores of Derwentwater as well.

It is not clear which exact route Coleridge took from Coniston to the outskirts of Ambleside where he spent the last night of his walk. The only source of information is his *Notebook* entry, which is singularly confusing:

> ... about 2 miles from Coniston just where Hawkshead and Esthwaite with Priest-pot and its floating Isle with Trees, then at the farther end (nearest Esthwaite) 15 yards long – there there is on your left, belonging to one John Swainson, with a compleate colonnade of clipped yews – an old man with his wife – had small else to do – was a Tanner, but long given over – has children, his they are grown up and married off – some time before this I came upon the view of Wyndermere – ....

This is the last of the notes he made during the walk. The 'Priest-pot' he mentions is a small stretch of water just north of Esthwaite Water.

Coleridge was now in country that must have reminded

him at every turn of his absent friend Wordsworth. It was here, at Hawkshead, that the young Wordsworth had been sent to school. In these hills he had roamed at large and felt the enveloping power of nature – skating on the lakes, setting snares for woodcock at night, climbing the crags to get birds' eggs.

It is all described with incomparable power in the first two books of Wordsworth's poem 'The Prelude', which he wrote during the bitter winter of 1798–9. The poem's sub-title is 'Growth of a Poet's Mind' and it was originally intended to accompany a much grander, philosophical poem which Coleridge had been urging his friend to write and which was to be called 'The Recluse'. In the event, 'The Recluse' was never completed. 'The Prelude' was, however, and there are many, including me, who see it as the pinnacle of Wordsworth's achievement. Astonishingly, it was never published during his life. He worked at it continually, revising and rewriting, and there are now three quite distinct versions – those of 1799, 1805 and 1850. Many readers, once again including me, prefer the freshness of the first version:

> ... For I would walk alone
> In storm and tempest, or in starlight nights
> Beneath the quiet heavens, and at that time
> Would feel whate'er there is of power in sound
> To breathe an elevated mood, by form
> Or image unprofaned; and I would stand
> Beneath some rock, listening to sounds that are
> The ghostly language of the ancient earth,
> Or make their dim abode in distant winds.
> Thence did I drink the visionary power.

William and Dorothy Wordsworth always thought of 'The Prelude' as 'the poem for Coleridge'. It was written not just for him but to him, addressing him as 'my friend' and 'my brother'. It quotes from his 'Frost at Midnight' and uses images derived from his letters and conversation. Its central theme is one that was central to Coleridge's thinking too. In the first years of their friendship, for all the disparities in character, they were so close that it is impossible to disentangle the threads of thought and determine which of them originated which idea. Coleridge had read the two first books of 'The Prelude', in manuscript, or had them read to him and, although he continued to press Wordsworth to turn his attention to the philosophical poem, it reinforced his conviction that his friend's poetic powers were growing while his own were waning.

There is a further reason why Coleridge's mind, as he moved on towards Ambleside, must have been full of these memories and thoughts. He had walked this way with Words-worth less than three years earlier, when he was being introduced to the Lake District.

I set off from Coniston in a light but steady drizzle. I always seem to be unlucky with the weather around there. As usual, the surrounding hills and mountains were obliterated by mist, and all the passing cars had their headlights on.

It is a short day's walk over easy ground so I made a slight detour to revisit Tarn Hows, perhaps the District's most popular beauty spot. It is reckoned that some three-quarters of a million people go there each year, and climb out of their cars and coaches to picnic by the lake or stroll along its gravel paths, admiring the prospect. Undeniably, it is a pretty place, in the chocolate box manner; the great majority of its visitors are charmed and delighted. Equally undeniably, it feels oddly out of place in the Lake District.

The appearance of the valleys and fells of the District has been much modifed by man – farmhouses and barns, dry-stone walls, signs of mining and quarrying, the bare hillsides revealed when the forests came down. Tarn Hows, however, has taken this to extremes. It is completely man-made. Originally it was a group of muddy ponds among the trees. Some time during the nineteenth century a dam was built to raise the water level and create a single stretch of water. Paths were laid to it and around it. Later, when it was bequeathed to the National Trust, a large car park was added. There are always cars and people there, and in holiday periods they are there in their thousands.

Norman Nicholson said it looked like 'a wide-screen setting for *Rose Marie*'. In the distance, on a clear day, you can see the unmistakable craggy tops of the Langdale Pikes beyond, and they make Tarn Hows seem inappropriate. It would be perfectly acceptable as part of some nobleman's landscaped gardens or in the municipal park of a great city, but in the Lake District it feels artificial and tamed and somehow wrong.

As I dropped down towards Hawkshead I came across something I had seen nowhere else on the walk. A farmer's sign warned that the field fence was electrified; children and dogs should be kept under control.

Hawkshead used to be one of the most intriguing and evocative places in the Lake District. In Tudor times it was a wool-processing town and very prosperous. It grew hurriedly and haphazardly as tiny mills, weaving rooms, cottages and warehouses were built. One visitor in the 1950s, Frank Singleton – the man, incidentally, who, as Editor of the *Bolton Evening News*, gave me my first job – called it 'the strangest Chinese puzzle of a little town'. A few years later Norman Nicholson said, 'The whole village could be fitted into the boundaries of a large agricultural show; yet it contains enough corners, angles, alleys and entries to keep the eye happy for hours'. Wordsworth grew up there and always remembered it with deep affection as 'that beloved vale'. From the top of a steep little hill, the fifteenth-century church presides over a complex huddle of lanes and alleyways, shops and cottages and the Elizabethan 'Free Grammar School' where you can see the initials 'WW' firmly carved in a desk-top.

It is difficult to believe now but, according to W. G. Collingwood, a reliable and sharp-eyed witness, the sad transformation of Hawkshead had already started at the beginning of this century. In his book *The Lake Counties*, first published in 1902, he complained that the character of the village was being undermined:

> ... tasteless restoration has stripped the homely rough-cast from the church and coarsely pointed it over. Wordsworth's Yew is gone. Flag Street also will be looked for in vain; where the beck ran down between the houses now there is only a somewhat squalid alley with a sewer under it, considered by the authorities to

be more sanitary. We are not yet quite clever enough in these matters to do the needful cleansing and restoration without destroying the old landmarks and the old rustic charm, and Hawkshead is being modernised.

One shudders to think what Collingwood, or even worse, Wordsworth, would say if they could see the place today. It has been pedestrianised and prettified and petrified almost. Traffic is banned from the narrow, twisting lanes, and a vast car park has been created a few yards from the heart of the village. There is a constant queue of vehicles jostling to get in or out, a constant stream of people hurrying to and fro. Everywhere you turn you find pubs and cafés, tea shops and souvenir shops and woollen shops and sheepskin shops, all sprucely painted and carefully designed to make the most of their 'olde worlde' quaintness. The whole place, it seems, has abandoned itself to the need to separate tourists from their money.

Hawkshead lies within 2 miles of the western shores of Windermere. It is here that the impact of tourism on the Lake District has been most ferociously felt. In fact this is where it all began, when Mr English started to build his circular house on Belle Isle in 1774 – 'the first house,' according to Wordsworth, 'that was built in the Lake District for the sake of the beauty of the country'.

Several factors have been at work. The first is simply geographical. Windermere is the most southerly of the lakes and therefore the one most easily reached from the industrial and mercantile centres of Lancashire and Yorkshire, the Midlands and London. The most recent factors have been the arrival *en masse* of the motor car and the construction of fast motorways, bringing the Lake District within two hours' driving of concentrated centres of population. The other prime cause was the coming of the railway in the mid-nineteenth century, which led to the first organised movement to protect the District from alien intrusion and possible destruction. William Wordsworth – it is very hard, hereabouts, to get away from the man – played an active part in that.

Long before the railways became a threat, Wordsworth

was preaching the need for vigilance. In his *Guide to the Lake District*, first published in 1810, he expressed the hope that 'better taste should prevail among these new proprietors' in order to 'prevent unnecessary deviations from that path of simplicity and beauty along which, without design and unconsciously, their humble predecessors have moved'. He added, in a clarion call that has been seen as the origin of the notion of a national park:

> In this wish the author will be joined by persons of pure taste throughout the whole island, who, by their visits (often repeated) to the Lakes in the North of England, testify that they deem the district a sort of national property, in which every man has a right and interest who has an eye to perceive and a heart to enjoy.

At first, it was not the holiday visitors that worried Wordsworth but the untutored rich who came to build holiday homes in the District. This changed in the mid-1840s when the railway mania, sweeping the country, threatened to reach into Lakeland.

In 1844 plans were announced for the extension of the railway from Oxenholme, near Kendal, to a point just north of Bowness which is now Windermere town. Wordsworth was in his mid-seventies but hurled himself into battle. He wrote to Mr Gladstone, demanding his support. And he composed a powerful sonnet, which began:

> Is then no nook of English ground secure
> From rash assault? ...

Wordsworth, by this time, was a figure of national standing, whose words carried much weight. His sonnet was printed in the *Morning Post,* and he backed it up with two long letters which the paper published in December 1844. His arguments are sometimes rambling, but the main points are clear enough: the special and precious quality of the Lake District was 'its beauty and its character of seclusion and retirement'; the building of the railway line and the running of the trains would greatly disturb that; worst of all, the trains would bring into the District hordes of working-class people from the industrial regions who would not know how to appreciate what they found and might well destroy it. It was an unashamedly elitist argument. Wordsworth's politics had moved a very long way since the first days of the French Revolution when he had welcomed the downfall of the aristocracy.

He put his case forcefully. 'The humbler ranks of society,' he said, 'are not, and cannot be, in a state to gain material benefit from a more speedy access than they now have to this beautiful region'. He described what would happen:

> ... look, in the first place, at the little town of Bowness, in the event of such railway inundations. What would become of it in this, not the Retreat, but the Advance of the Ten Thousand? Leeds, I am told, has sent as many at once to Scarborough. We should have the whole of Lancashire, and no small part of Yorkshire, pouring in upon us to meet the men of Durham, and the borderers from Cumberland and Northumberland.

He did not say it, but he clearly shared Ruskin's fears about the invading factory workers: 'I do not want them to see Helvellyn when they are drunk'.

Despite Wordsworth's efforts, and those of an organised pressure group, the railway came to the lakeside, and a new Victorian town was quickly created, Windermere. They wanted to extend the line to Ambleside, Rydal and Grasmere, but that was not permitted.

Wordsworth's fears about the effects of the 'inundations' on Bowness and the surrounding region proved well-founded. The north-eastern shores of the lake became the scene of intensive urban and semi-urban development. The twentieth century has multiplied the damage with its motor cars and coaches, car parks and caravans, caravan sites and campsites, motor boats and water-skiers. Windermere is not only the largest of the lakes, it is also the busiest and the noisiest and by far the most polluted.

The biggest threat facing the Lake District arises from the fact that it is altogether too popular. Too many people want houses there and this pushes up the prices and makes it difficult for the locals, especially the young. And too many people like to visit the District, some 13 million a year, they say. The numbers increase and the holiday season gets longer, so that the very things that make the place special and precious are inexorably eroded. It is a small and highly vulnerable area. 'Each man,' Oscar Wilde said, 'kills the thing he loves.' The Lake District is in danger of being loved to death.

There are, after all, many resorts in Britain, and an increasing number in Europe and along the shores of the Mediterranean, which cater for those who want to spend their holidays with thousands of like-minded people, engulfed in candy floss and popular music, surrounded by bars and amusement parks and one-armed bandits and bingo halls. It seems only fair that some places should be preserved for those others who prefer comparative peace and solitude, escape from everyday routines and pressures, closer contact with the natural world, the chance to stretch their muscles and their minds in fresh air and freedom – all the things, in fact, that Coleridge found on his 'circumcursion'.

CHAPTER TEN

Homeward Bound

Coleridge's eighth day was a short one. He could easily have walked on as far as Grasmere, but an old acquaintance of his, Charles Lloyd, had a spacious home at Clappersgate near Ambleside, so he stayed there on the last night of his walk.

Lloyd was a strange and sometimes difficult man. He was three years Coleridge's junior, the son of a wealthy Midlands banker. He had youthful aspirations to be a poet so, in 1796, he was sent to live with the Coleridge family in Bristol as a 'pupil-lodger', presumably in the hope that some of the older man's genius would rub off on the younger. It did not work out like that. Lloyd was sensitive, moody and subject to epileptic fits. Coleridge's tempestuous company was hardly likely to have a calming effect on such a companion. Back home in 1798, Lloyd wrote a novel, *Edmund Oliver,* in which he portrayed his former teacher as irresponsible and impetuous, living in an opium-induced confusion. The book is all but unreadable today, but Coleridge read it and was hurt by it.

By August 1802 his resentment must have subsided. Certainly, Charles Lloyd's situation had greatly improved. He had married a charming young woman called Sophia, begun a family, and acquired a country home on the banks of the River Brathay. The place was then called Low Brathay. Today it is known as Old Brathay, and provides staff accommodation and offices for an outdoor pursuits centre.

Coleridge gives no account of his stay there, but there is no reason to doubt that he was welcomed and well looked after. Lloyd was a happy man at this stage of his life, and was already starting to build up a reputation for lavish hospitality. His home was becoming the focal point for a cultured and lively group – writers, artists and musicians. This was the best period in his troubled life. Later, his mental and nervous disorders were to return with renewed force. In 1816 he had to be taken away to an asylum for the insane.

The final day of Coleridge's walk was almost as long as the first, some 16 miles. The route was well-known to him, and full of memories. It was then, as it is today, the sole north–south road through the centre of the Lake District. It was pleasant going when he did it, though undemanding, but it is not to be recommended to modern walkers. Sometimes you can find quieter side roads and paths, but for much of the way there is no alternative but to walk along the edge of the A591 with the traffic roaring past continuously in both directions. You meet very few pedestrians here.

The first part of the journey is not too bad. Just beyond Clappersgate, I was able to leave the main road and follow the winding lane along the western bank of the River Rothay. Ahead lay the heart of Wordsworth-land – the adjoining, enclosed and totally distinctive little vales of Rydal and Grasmere. Thomas Gray described Grasmere rapturously when he passed through in 1769:

> . . . from the shore a low promontory pushes itself far into the water, and on it stands a white village with the Parish Church rising in the midst of it, hanging enclosures, corn-fields, and meadows green as an emerald with their trees and hedges and cattle fill up the whole space from the edge of the water. Just opposite to you is a large farm-house at the bottom of a steep smooth lawn embosomed in old woods, which climb half way up the mountain's side, and discover above them a broken line of crags, that crown the scene. Not a single red tile, no flaming Gentleman's house, or garden-walls break in upon the repose of this little unsuspected paradise, but all is peace, rusticity and happy poverty in its neatest most becoming attire.

A few years after that visit the schoolboy Wordsworth, roaming far from Hawkshead, peeped over the ridge and was enchanted by the same prospect:

... Alone and devious from afar he came;
And, with a sudden influx overpowered
At sight of this seclusion, he forgot
His haste, for hasty had his footsteps been
As boyish his pursuits; and sighing said,
'What happy fortune were it here to live!
And, if a thought of dying, if a thought
Of mortal separation could intrude
With paradise before him, here to die!'

In 1799 he did go and live in Grasmere, and half a century later he died above the waters of Rydal. It was here that he enjoyed his most creative years, raised his family, and saw his fame increase as his poetic power declined.

More than 20 years after Wordsworth's death in 1850, Canon Rawnsley, who had been posted to a living on the northern shores of Windermere, had the bright notion of talking to the older folk hereabouts and getting their memories of the great man who had lived among them so long. The result was the most entertaining of the Canon's many articles, which he called 'Reminiscences of Wordsworth among the peasantry of Westmoreland', first published in 1882.

Everyone he spoke to remembered 'Wudsworth', as they all called him, as a man very much apart – austere in manner, taciturn, very simple in dress and general lifestyle, self-contained and calm. He was never one of them. He would consort with 'the quality' but not with the common folk. He walked about the lanes daily but never spoke to anyone he passed. He talked to himself, though, a great deal, working away at the lines of some new poem. Children were frightened when they suddenly heard his deep voice from behind a hedge or round a corner. By all accounts, he was not fond of children or animals, and he hated cats. He also hated to see things changed – trees being felled or large boulders removed.

None of the locals had any regard for his poetry. Some believed that Dorothy did the bulk of the writing; others that Coleridge's son, Hartley, kept him secretly provided with verses. Most of them were sure that Hartley – a great favourite because he did a lot of drinking and chatting with them – was by far the better writer. His poems were more readily understood and often funny.

One man, asked about Wordsworth's poetry, said, 'He was nowt to li'le Hartley'. Another, who had delivered butter to the Wordsworth house as a lad, described the elderly Wordsworth as a man who never laughed and very rarely smiled:

> . . . a man as hed nea pleasure in his face . . . a desolate-minded man, ye kna. Queer thing that, mun, but it was his hobby, ye kna. It was potry as did it. . . . It was a queer thing, but it would like eneugh cause him to be desolate . . . You cud tell fra t' man's faace his potry wad nivver hev nea laugh in it.

I was reminded of these revelations when I passed the solid, four-square house called Fox How, which stands in green and leafy grounds between the lane and the river. It was built, very much according to Wordsworth's architectural advice, by his friend, Dr Thomas Arnold, the famous headmaster of Rugby School. It was his admiration for Wordsworth that first brought Dr Arnold to the Lake District. Despite differences of opinion on many religious and political issues – Arnold was a reformer, Wordsworth an entrenched reactionary by this time – they enjoyed each other's company. Soon, Arnold wanted a holiday home in the region. Wordsworth negotiated the purchase of the estate and, to a large extent, presided over the building. Fox How was constructed in the early 1830s. More than 40 years later, one of Canon Rawnsley's informants, who had been a waller by trade, told him:

> I can mind he [Wordsworth] and the Doctor had girt argiments aboot the chimleys time we was building Foxhow, and Wudsworth sed he liked a bit o' colour in 'em. And that the chimley coigns sud be natural headed and natural bedded, a lile bit red and a lile bit yallar. For there is a bit of colour i' t' quarry stean up Easedale way. And he-ed a girt fancy an' aw for chim-

leys square up hauf way, and round t'other. And so
we built 'em that road.

For Dr Arnold, the house was a refuge from the intense
pressures of his working life. He came to love it almost too
much for his ethical comfort. It was, he said, 'a home so peaceful
and delightful that it would not be right to make it one's constant
portion'.

Fox How is a spacious house in a splendid position. The
Doctor's nine children, including Matthew who was to become
a well-known poet and critic, enjoyed their holidays there. One
of his grand-daughters, Mary Augusta, spent the greater part of
her childhood there, running freely about the fells, and grew up
to become the best-selling novelist of the late-Victorian years
under her married name, Mrs Humphry Ward. Dr Arnold died
in 1842, but the family retained possession of Fox How until
1923 when the youngest of his daughters died at the age of 90.
Among the visitors to the house were Harriet Martineau from
Ambleside and her friend Charlotte Brontë, and many of those
Huxleys and Trevelyans and Arnold-Fosters who married into
the Arnold clan and influenced so many aspects of British life
and thought in the closing decades of the nineteenth century.

This region must be the richest in the Lake District for
eminent literary associations. Harriet Martineau's house, The
Knoll, is across the valley. Less than a mile further on is Rydal
Mount, which was Wordsworth's home for the last 37 years of
his life. Just beyond that, by the main road, stands Nab Cottage
where De Quincey lived for a while and where, some years later,
'li'le' Hartley Coleridge lived and died. And then you come to
Grasmere which contains three of the Wordsworth homes as
well as the family graves, and which thrives today very largely
on the Wordsworth name.

In 1802 Dove Cottage, the first and by far the happiest of
their Grasmere homes, was on the main road. Coleridge called
there on his way through, though he knew his friends were still
in France. He conducted himself with great delicacy. In the letter
he wrote to Sara Hutchinson next day, he said:

> I slept at Bratha on Sunday Night – and did not go on to Grasmere, tho' I had time enough, and was not over-fatigued; but tho' I have no objection to sleep in a lonely House, I did not like to sleep in *their* lonely lonely House. I called the next day – went into the garden – pulled some Peas, and shelled and drest them, and eat them for my dinner with one rasher of Bacon boiled – but I did not go up stairs, not indeed anywhere but the Kitchen. Partly I was very wet and my boots very dirty – and Molly had set the Pride of her Heart upon its niceness – and still more – I had small desire to go up!

From here his route took him over the pass of Dunmail Raise; past the pile of stones that is said to mark the grave of an Anglo-Saxon tribal ruler called King Dunmail who was, according to legend, killed in a battle here in the tenth century; then down to Thirlmere.

Here, memories of his friends must have flooded into his mind. The Wordsworths had often walked to Thirlmere from Dove Cottage, while Coleridge walked southwards from Keswick, to meet and chat and picnic at some halfway point. In her *Journal* Dorothy described one such day, 4th May 1802:

> ... We saw Coleridge on the Wytheburn side of the water. He crossed the Beck to us. Mr. Simpson was fishing there. William and I ate a luncheon, then went on towards the waterfall. It is a glorious wild solitude under that lofty purple crag. It stood upright by itself .... We climbed the hill but looked in vain for a shade except at the foot of the great waterfall, and there we did not like to stay on account of the loose stones above our heads. We came down and rested upon a moss-covered Rock, rising out of the bed of the River. There we lay, ate our dinner and stayed there till about 4 o'clock or later. Wm and C. repeated and read verses. I drank a little Brandy and water and was in Heaven .... We parted from Coleridge at Sara's Crag after having looked at the letters which C. carved in the

morning. I kissed them all. Wm deepened the T with
C.'s penknife. We sate afterwards on the wall, seeing
the sun go down and the reflections in the still water.
C. looked well and parted from us chearfully, hopping
up upon the side stones.

What Dorothy refers to as 'Sara's Crag' later came to be more
widely known as 'the Rock of Names'. It was a large boulder,
on the smooth face of which Coleridge and Wordsworth had
incised the initials, in letters more than an inch high, of their
group of close friends: WW; MH (Mary Hutchinson); DW
(Dorothy); STC; JW (John Wordsworth, the sailor brother);
and SH (Sara Hutchinson).

Coleridge loved Thirlmere. More than a year later, after
walking home from Grasmere, he wrote in his *Notebook*:

> O Thirlmere! – let me somehow or other celebrate the
> world in thy mirror. Conceive all possible varieties of
> Form, Fields and Trees, and naked or ferny Crags –
> ravines, behaired with Birches – Cottages, smoking
> chimneys, dazzling *wet* places of small rock-preci-
> pices – dazzling castle windows in the reflection – all
> these, within a divine outline in a mirror of three miles
> distinct vision! – and the distance closed in by the
> Reflection of Raven Crag, which at every bemisting of
> the mirror by gentle motion became a perfect vast
> Castle Tower, the corners rounded and pillar'd or
> fluted ... All this in bright lightest yellow, yellow-
> green, green, crimson, and orange! – The single Birch
> Trees hung like Tresses of Sea Weed – the Cliffs like
> organ pipes! – and when a little Breath of Air spread
> a delicious Network over the Lake, all these colours
> seemed then to float on, like the reflections of the
> rising or setting Sun.

I doubt if any other valley in the district, not even Ennerdale, has been transformed so completely as Thirlmere. The
early descriptions are full of praise. Father Thomas West spoke

of its contrasts and variety, and added: 'Its singular beauty is its being almost intersected in the middle by two peninsulas, that are joined by a bridge, in a taste suitable to the genius of the place'. Thomas Gray described the lake as 'narrow and about three miles long, resembling a river in its course; little shining torrents hurry down the rocks to join it, with not a bush to overshadow them, or cover their march'. And Harriet Martineau, in her *Description of the English Lakes* (1858), strongly recommended visitors to take the less-frequented path along the western shores of the lake:

> The stranger leaves the mail road within a mile of the Nag's Head, passes the cottages called by the boastful name of the City of Wythburn, and a few farm-houses, and soon emerging from the fences, finds himself on a grassy level under the Armboth Fells, within an amphitheatre of rocks, with the lake before him, and Helvellyn beyond, overshadowing it. The rocks behind are feathered with wood, except where a bold crag here, and a free cataract there, introduces a variety. There is a clear pool in the midst of the grass, where, if the approaching tread be light, the heron may be seen fishing, or faithfully reflected in the mirror.

It would be impossible today to recognise the valley from these accounts. Helvellyn is still the presiding mountain but in other respects the variety of the scene has been replaced with uniformity, its cheerful lights and shades by a general air of gloom. The lake no longer resembles a river, nor is it virtually cut in two by the peninsulas. The slopes on either side are clothed in conifers, all the same height and colour, set in straight lines. Most people nowadays drive quickly past, sparing Thirlmere no more than a glance or two.

The great change occurred in the last quarter of the last century. The factories and the increasing number of people in and around Manchester needed more water. They wanted it as pure as possible and from a source high enough to reduce the pumping charges. Their search led them, inevitably, to Thirlmere. By 1877 Manchester Waterworks Committee had bought the lake and its surrounding hillsides. Two years later Parliament passed an Act empowering them to dam the lake at its northern end and install enough pipelines and pumping machinery to extract 50 million gallons a day. The work started.

A Thirlmere Defence Association was formed. Many leading figures, including Thomas Carlyle and William Morris, gave their support. John Ruskin, now living at Coniston, denounced the scheme and cried, 'Manchester is plotting to steal the waters of Thirlmere and the clouds of Helvellyn'. Someone wrote to the *Westmorland Gazette* saying, 'Avaunt, ye votaries of Mammon! – ye artisans unwashed! Keep to your industries, and leave us our sublime scenery'. It was all in vain. Thirlmere became a reservoir. The level of the lake was raised by 50 feet, drowning many cottages and some farms. Conifers were planted all round to preserve the slopes from erosion. Solid stone walls and fences were constructed to keep sheep and people out. A motor road was built along the western shore, and on the eastern side, below the A591, they erected a pumping station, designed in the heaviest Victorian mock-Gothic style.

In a few years the valley was so transformed that W. G. Collingwood was moved to write:

> Thirlmere has no expanse, but it once was the richest in story and scenery of all the lakes. The old charm of its shores has quite vanished, and the sites of its legends are hopelessly altered, so that the walk along either side is a mere sorrow to anyone who cared for it before; the sham castles are an outrage and the formality of the roads, beloved of cyclists, deforms the hillsides like a scar on a face.

The Manchester engineers even blew up the 'Rock of Names'. Canon H. D. Rawnsley, who had not played an active part in the conservation battle because he appreciated the city's great need for water, was outraged when he heard of this. He and his wife went to the spot, found the carved fragments and set them in a cairn, just above the A591 road. The cairn remained there for nearly a century, until 1984 when the North-West Water Authority handed the fragments over to the Dove Cottage

Trust in Grasmere. They can now be seen, set into the face of a boulder in the garden behind the Wordsworth Museum.

The Water Authority had taken Thirlmere over from Manchester Corporation but was still bound by the provisions of the Act of 1879, and this led to a remarkable 'David and Goliath' confrontation in 1985. Mrs Susan Johnson of Ravenglass, daughter of the man who saved Eskdale and Dunnerdale from excessive afforestation in the 1930s, brought a private prosecution against the Authority. The Act laid down that whoever ran the reservoir should always pay 'reasonable regard to the beauty of the scenery in general', and that the lake shore areas in particular should be planted with native trees – oak and ash, birch and alder – and not exclusively with alien conifers like the spruce. The Authority, Mrs Johnson said, had ignored these injunctions.

The case was heard by the Keswick magistrates in January 1985. On the one side stood Mrs Johnson, aged 67; on the other, the solicitor and assorted experts of the Water Authority. When the solicitor asked whom she represented, she said: 'I'm a one-man band. I am bringing this case in the interests of the public ... all those who go to the hills and enjoy our landscape'. She had prepared her case carefully, backed it up with maps and documents, and the magistrates came down on her side. 'The Water Authority,' they said, 'has not acted reasonably'. The Authority promised that in future the forest edges, along the lake shore and public roads and paths, would be softened and varied by the planting of broadleaf trees and native shrubs.

This century has brought further and even more brutal exploitation of the lakes for reservoirs, most notably at Haweswater in the eastern fells. It is unlikely, however, that there will be more depredations of this kind. The dispiriting examples of Thirlmere and Haweswater are there for all to see. And the environmental pressure groups are sufficiently powerful now – as they showed in 1980–1 over the plans to get more water from Ennerdale and Wastwater – to make sure it does not happen again.

The main road along the eastern shore of Thirlmere makes for weary walking, with fast traffic roaring by continuously.

Fortunately it is possible to get off the road for 3 miles or so and follow a forest track higher up the fellside. It is an undulating path, with stout wooden bridges across the many gullies. You walk on a yielding surface of pine needles. There was no one else there when I walked along, and no sign of any wildlife. Apart from the faint hum of the passing traffic lower down, there was no sound. I am no lover of these great conifer forests; I think them out of place and disfiguring in the valleys of the Lake District, but they are not altogether deplorable. There is something about the deep silence and stillness of them, the keen scent of resin in the air, the all-enveloping trees, that creates a strange and distinctive and very strong atmosphere. It is another world entirely, and one that strikes chords deep in the subconscious of anyone brought up on the fairytales of the Brothers Grimm.

As I dropped down to rejoin the road, once more on open ground, my thoughts were shattered by the sudden, deafening roar of a military aircraft flying northwards at great speed and well below the regulation minimum altitude of 250 feet. For the first eight and a half days of my walk I had been spared this modern horror. This is unusual. All year round, when visibility is good, scarcely a day passes without the peace and quiet being destroyed by the passage of jet planes, shrieking out of nowhere and shredding the air immediately above your head as they go. It is even more startling when you are high up on a steep slope and they zoom through below your boots. Some people still think of the Lake District as wilderness country, but nowadays it is rarely possible to walk for more than two or three hours without coming across some – usually unpleasant – reminder of the twentieth century.

Coleridge arrived back at Greta Hall at 8 p.m. on Monday, 9th August, to find the family well, the boys delighted to see him, and a pile of letters. That night he sat down at his desk to write to his brother-in-law Robert Southey, whom he had been trying to persuade to come and live in Keswick and share Greta Hall with them. Coleridge began his letter with a brief account of his nine-day walk, which concluded with the words:

> ... this morning walked from Bratha to Grasmere,
> and from Grasmere to Greta Hall – where I now am,
> quite sweet and ablute, and have but even now read
> thro' your Letter – which I will answer by the night's
> post, and therefore must defer all account of my very
> Interesting Tour – saying only that of all earthly things
> which I have beheld, the view of Sca'fell and *from*
> Sca'Fell, (*both* views from its own summit) is the most
> heart-exciting.

'Ablute' is an odd word, and for a long time I thought, even
hoped, that it might have been a misprint for 'absolute'. It was
good to imagine Coleridge sitting in his study and feeling 'sweet
and absolute', pleasantly tired from his walk but fit and well,
fulfilled and serene, not a common condition with him. Unfortunately I now believe the word is correct, and that he meant
nothing more than that he had taken off his walking clothes,
had a good wash – perhaps even a bath – and put on clean
clothing.

The next evening he wrote to Sara Hutchinson, beginning
'My dearest Sara' and ending 'Bless you, my Darling!' He apolo-
gises for not finishing his 'Great-sheet Letter' describing the
walk and says he will do so 'as soon as possible'. He never got
round to it. In this letter, among many other things, he says:

> ... I am well, and have had a very delightful and
> feeding Excursion, or rather Circumcursion ... In the
> course of my Tour (and I was absent 9 days) I gave
> away to Bairns and foot-sore Wayfarers four shillings
> and some odd pence; and I *spent* nine shillings – sum
> total, £0 13s 0d – but to this must be added the wear
> and tear of my Boots, which are gone to be mended;
> and sixpence for a great knee-patch for my Pantaloons,
> which will not however be worn an hour the shorter
> time for the said large knee-patch. I have now *no*
> *clothes but what are patched at the elbows, and knees,*
> *and in the seat* – and I am determined to wear them
> *out and out* – and to have none till after Christmas.

My nine-day excursion cost me just over £200 altogether. Whenever I could I stayed at bed and breakfast places, which were all good and remarkably cheap (between £10 and £12). But on three nights I was unable to find cheap accommodation and had to book into hotels. They were perfectly comfortable too, but more than twice the price. One evening I treated myself to a good restaurant meal. For the rest, I lived sparingly on beer and simple bar meals. I gave nothing away to passing beggars because there were none. This was one of the great differences between Coleridge's walk and mine. In his day the villages and the country lanes were full of homeless and derelict people, sometimes whole families on the move, the victims of personal misfortune or enclosures or the decline in cottage industries or their own mismanagement. Their numbers had been swelled by the long years of fighting the French; many wounded soldiers and sailors, disbanded and discarded by an ungrateful government, could only survive by begging. Dorothy Wordsworth's *Journal* mentions them with painful frequency.

I was surprised by this enormous difference in cost, even allowing for the fact that Coleridge certainly did not have to pay for his last night at Brathay and probably was not charged for his first night at Long Moor. Not quite 200 years later, my journey cost more than 400 times as much as Coleridge's had done.

CHAPTER ELEVEN

Afterthoughts

For me, as for Coleridge, the final day was showery and I was glad to get home and have a bath and change into fresh, clean clothing. I was happy to have completed the 'circumcursion', even happier to think that I would not need to do it again. It is not a route to be recommended to walkers. Too much of it, especially on the north–south reaches, takes you along busy main roads, with no escape from the sounds and smells of traffic.

The nine days had been made fascinating for me by my interest in Coleridge. It was fun trying to find the exact route he took, especially when his descriptions were vague or ambiguous. It was interesting to sit, with his words in front of me, and look at all the things that were there, virtually the same, when he walked that way – the tumbling streams and waterfalls, the ruined sheepfold on Floutern Pass and the boat-house by the edge of Devoke Water, the craggy summit of Scafell, the wide views of rolling fells and ridges stretching into the distance. A lot has happened to the Lake District in 200 years, not all of it good, but the unique magic of the place – the quality that made Coleridge's spirit soar – is still potent.

More than once, in the weeks after I returned to Keswick, I was asked whether I had felt, at any time on the journey, that Coleridge was with me. In one sense, of course, he was with me throughout, at the forefront of my mind. I carried photocopies of the relevant pages of his letters and his *Notebook*, and consulted them frequently. I looked out for the things he mentioned and read his descriptions of them, admiring the vigour and the accuracy and the aptness of his imagery. I am sorry to have to confess, however, that I never felt that he was present in any stronger sense than that. I only wish I had.

The journey brought no major discoveries. I found the 'four-foot stone' in Eskdale, but failed to find it anything like so fascinating as Coleridge had done. I had been a little surprised by his lack of interest in the old churches that he walked past, the remains of the Roman fort at Hardknott, the ruins of Calder Abbey. It was interesting, and something of a tribute to the calm and continuity of Lake District life, that five of the eight houses he slept in are still there and in use, most of them looking much as they must have done in 1802, though a little more weathered now. The other three places may have survived as well, but since he did not say exactly where he slept at St Bees and Egremont and Ulpha Bridge it is impossible to tell. I knew, before I set off, that there had been considerable inflation in Britain in the past 200 years, but was rather shocked to find that the cost of fell-walking had risen so much.

There was a negative surprise, too. I had always supposed that there was more abundant animal life in the fells in those days and that it would have been more visible. The old guide-books speak of mammals – wild cats, polecats, pine martens – that lived in the mountains then, though they have long disappeared now. There were also, as there still are, red deer and roe deer and foxes. You rarely see them today, of course – I saw none on my walk – because they have a well-founded distrust of human beings and there are many of us in the hills these days, usually making a noise. But there were very few people about when Coleridge did his walk. He was alone and probably moved quietly. He often stopped to survey the scene. Yet he reported no sighting of any mammal. He was interested in all forms of wildlife, so I feel sure he would have kept a sharp eye out and that he would have mentioned it in his *Notebook* or his letters had he seen anything. Perhaps he was just unlucky.

Only once does he mention birds – the angry 'sea fowl' that made him feel unwelcome at Devoke Water. That is, perhaps, not so surprising. There are probably more birds about now, certainly at the higher levels, than there were then. In the eighteenth century the big, predatory birds – eagles, falcons, ravens and carrion crows – were thought to be a menace to new-born lambs. They were shot and trapped and discouraged from breeding – stout ropes were kept in most valleys so that men could be lowered down the cliff-faces to smash the nests. In the latter part of the twentieth century, when green became the fashionable ideological colour, strenuous efforts have been made – with considerable success – to lure these birds back. In the nesting season a 24-hour watch is now kept on eagles and peregrine falcons to protect them from human predators.

For the most part, what I learned from the walk was what I had expected to learn. I feared it was going to be harder for me to find accommodation each evening than it had been for Coleridge, and so it proved, though my only serious difficulty was on the first night. I also knew, before I set off, what the main change to the region was. It can be stated simply. In 1802 the Lake District was an overwhelmingly pastoral society, centred on the Herdwick sheep. The Herdwick are still there today and they have been joined, on the lower ground, by other breeds and cross-breeds of sheep. But the primary concern of most Lakeland people nowadays is with a very different creature, one that is both more demanding and more profitable, the tourist.

Broadly speaking, the higher you go in the fells the less changed is the landscape. Even so, on the highest ridges and in the wildest weather, you will almost always come across other walkers. The sport that Coleridge created in the opening years of the last century has become immensely popular.

A little lower down, on the hillsides, the appearance of the landscape has been affected by two chief factors: the spreading of bracken, and the planting of conifers. Lower still, at lake level, some valleys have been transformed by the creation of reservoirs.

But the biggest changes have been caused by the rapid and continuing growth of the tourist trade, whose effects are most visible, most audible, and most deplorable, in the valley bottoms. There are tarmacdamed roads and car parks; caravan parks and campsites; filling stations, public lavatories and information centres. In the towns – such as Ambleside and Grasmere and Keswick – there are large hotels and small hotels and scores of boarding houses; restaurants and cafés and tea rooms; pubs in which all hope of rational conversation is destroyed by obligatory canned music played at a high-decibel level; take-away food shops; art galleries and museums of many kinds; parks with children's playgrounds and miniature golf; innumerable souvenir shops and sweater shops and climbers' shops and pot shops and Beatrix Potter shops and shops where visitors can buy Kendal Mint Cake and Cumberland rum butter and 'original' gingerbread and postcards galore. There is strong pressure – from developers and entrepreneurs who put short-term profit above considerations of long-term and irreparable damage – to push the District ever further down this road.

If Coleridge could see the Lake District today he would certainly be astonished by the changes that have taken place. He would, I imagine, be delighted to find that so many people have followed his example in seeking escape and adventure and exaltation in the high fells. He would also, I suspect, find himself appalled by the clamour and noise and sheer vulgarity of much that has been allowed to happen lower down.

Nearly five years before he made his 'circumcursion', when he was thinking of becoming a minister in the Unitarian church, Coleridge went to Shrewsbury to preach and took for his text the New Testament words: 'And he went up into the mountain to pray, himself, alone'. This was January 1798. We know about it because the young William Hazlitt was in the congregation. He had walked 10 miles through the cold and the mud to be there, but he was magnificently rewarded. The eloquence of the visiting preacher astonished him 'as if the sounds had echoed from the bottom of the human heart, and as if that prayer might have floated in solemn silence through the universe'. He described the experience, many years later, in an essay called 'My First Acquaintance with Poets'. The sermon, he goes on to say, was a sustained and powerful diatribe against war, which may have been appropriate to the times but hardly seems to derive directly from the text.

The New Testament words, nonetheless, stand as an excellent epigraph for the story of the 'circumcursion'. In August 1802 Coleridge went up into the mountains. He was alone. And, in a sense, he prayed. While he stretched his muscles and his limbs, and rejoiced in the adventure of it all, his mind was ever active. And such was the cast of Coleridge's mind that when he was talking to himself, he was, in effect, talking to God, looking for clues and keys to the beneficent unity of all creation, which he did not doubt.

Whenever he was excited or uplifted, Coleridge invoked the name of God, and he uttered one unmistakable prayer immediately after his dangerous descent of Broad Stand and the passing overhead of the thunderstorm:

> O God! what thoughts were mine! O how I wished
> for Health and Strength that I might wander about for
> a Month together, in the stormiest month of the year,
> among these Places, so lonely and savage and full of
> sounds!

The prayer was not answered. On his return home, the old troubles began to close in on him and, although there were some periods of respite, they intensified as the months passed.

He went on fell-walking. Charles and Mary Lamb arrived on the Greta Hall doorstep, unannounced, and stayed for three weeks. Coleridge escorted them up Skiddaw and took them on a tour of the local waterfalls.

Mrs Coleridge was not so welcoming to the visitors, however, and when they had gone the old domestic discord resurfaced. Coleridge wrote to a friend of 'Ill-tempered Speeches sent after me when I went out of the House, ill-tempered Speeches on my return, my friends received with freezing looks, the least opposition or contradiction occasioning screams of passion ....'

He was frequently sick, with a variety of ailments – turbulent guts, asthma, swellings, the old rheumatics. He had increasing recourse to laudanum and the brandy bottle. When he tried to reduce the dosage he suffered terrible withdrawal symptoms. Sleep was elusive and, when it did come, often brought fearful nightmares.

His love for Sara Hutchinson was as strong as ever, and as tormenting. He and his wife made efforts to regain their former loving relationship, but they were all in vain. It is hard to believe the tactlessness, the sheer insensitivity of some of the things Coleridge said to her. In November 1802 he wrote to her from South Wales, urging her to try to love the people he loved, and adding: 'Heaven knows! it is without any feeling of Pride in myself, to say – that in sex, acquirements, and in the quantity and quality of natural endowments whether of Feeling, or of Intellect, you are the Inferior'.

A few weeks later, as the birth of their third child approached, he was still in Wales and wrote to say he thought it would be a good idea for her to get Sara Hutchinson to nurse her through the lying-in, 'because you will hardly have another opportunity of having her by yourself and to yourself, and of learning to know her, such as she really is'. Mrs Coleridge did not take the opportunity. As usual, Coleridge was not there when the child was born, just before Christmas. It was a girl this time and, compounding the confusion, they called her Sara.

Coleridge was away from home a great deal, often for many weeks at a time. He was, as ever, full of ideas for major works that never got started. He was writing poetry, but it was uninspired. He wrote many articles for the *Morning Post* – the story of 'the Beauty of Buttermere' had broken – but was unable to earn enough to dispel his perennial money troubles.

When his health allowed, he could still walk hard and far, relishing wild conditions. In January 1803 he walked northwards over the Kirkstone Pass and on to Grasmere in the teeth of a ferocious storm:

> I am no novice in mountain-mischiefs; but such a storm as this was I never witnessed, combining the intensity of the Cold, with the violence of the wind and rain. The rain-drops were pelted, or rather *slung*, against my face, by the Gusts, just like splinters of Flint; and felt as if every drop *cut* my flesh. My hands were all shrivelled up, like a washerwoman's; and so benumbed that I was obliged to carry my stick under my arm. O it was a wild business! Such hurry-scurry of Clouds, such volleys of sound!

The passage comes from a letter to his friend Thomas Wedgwood who had remonstrated with him for not turning back when he saw what the weather was like.

I have already, in Chapter Six, quoted a couple of sentences from Coleridge's reply, but I think it is worth giving his self-justification in full because it is the most sustained and comprehensive statement he ever made about what his fell-walking meant to him:

> You ask, in God's name, why I did not return when I saw the state of the weather? The true reason is simple, tho' it may be somewhat strange – the thought never once entered my head. The *cause* of this I suppose to be, that (I do not remember it at least) I never once in my whole life turned back in fear of the weather. Prudence is a plant, of which I, no doubt, possess some valuable specimens – but they are always in my hot-house, never out of the glasses – and least of all things would endure the climate of the mountains. In simple earnest, I never find myself alone within the embrace-ment of rocks and hills, a traveller up an alpine road, but my spirit courses, drives, and eddies, like a Leaf in Autumn: a wild activity, of thoughts, imaginations, feelings, and impulses of motion, rises up from within me – a sort of *bottom-wind*, that blows to no point of the compass, and comes from I know not whence, but agitates the whole of me; my whole Being is filled with waves, as it were, that roll and stumble, one this way, and one that way, like things that have no common master. I think that my soul must have pre-existed in the body of a Chamois-chaser; the simple image of the old object has been obliterated – but the feelings, and impulsive habits, and incipient actions, are in me, and the old scenery awakens them. The farther I ascend from animated Nature, from men, and cattle, and the common birds of the woods, and fields, the greater becomes in me the Intensity of the feeling of Life; Life seems to me then a universal spirit, that neither has, nor can have, an opposite. God is every where, I have exclaimed, and works every where; and where is there *room* for Death? In these moments it has been my creed, that Death exists only because

Ideas exist, that Life is limitless Sensation; that Death is a child of the organic senses, chiefly of the Sight; that Feelings die by flowing into the mould of the Intellect, and becoming Ideas; and that Ideas passing forth into action re-instate themselves again in the world of Life. And I do believe, that Truth lies inveloped in these loose generalisations. – I do not think it possible, that any bodily pains could eat out the love and joy, that is so substantially part of me, towards hills, and rocks, and steep waters!

In August 1803 he set off with William and Dorothy Wordsworth – William's first child had been born in June – for a six-week tour in Scotland. They took a one-horse 'jaunting car', a crude and not particularly comfortable vehicle that was wide open to the weather. Coleridge was once again in poor health and poor spirits. He diagnosed his ailment as 'Atonic Gout' and took with him plenty of what he called 'gout medicine', whatever that was. He hoped the trip would cure him of his various troubles.

Unfortunately the weather was bad and there was none of the joyful exchange of ideas and impressions that had marked their expeditions together in the Quantocks. Coleridge said Wordsworth was 'silent and self-centred'. Wordsworth later said that Coleridge had been 'in bad spirits, and somewhat too much in love with his own dejection'. When they reached the Loch Lomond region, Wordsworth suggested that they should separate, that Coleridge should walk back to Stirling and then get the coach home. Coleridge agreed, but as soon as he found himself alone, with no one else to think about or worry about, his spirits rose and he turned northwards instead and walked to Glencoe and then on to Fort William. His shoes were worn out and his feet were painful, but he wrote to his wife: '… nevertheless, I am enjoying myself, having Nature with solitude and liberty; the liberty natural and solitary, the solitude natural and free'.

From Fort William he walked to Fort Augustus, then across to Inverness, then south to Perth and Edinburgh, covering 263 miles in eight days (an average of nearly 33 miles a day). He could still walk with speed and great stamina, but there was something feverish about it now, driven almost, as if he were punishing his body and trying to obliterate his memories.

The year 1803 was the worst of his Lake District years, for his marriage, his health, his dependence on opiates, his inability to work. On 19th October he wrote in his *Notebook*:

> ... tomorrow my Birth Day, 31 years of age! – O me! my very heart dies! – This *year* has been one painful Dream – I have done nothing! – O for God's sake, let me whip and spur, so that Christmas may not pass without some thing having been done....

And later the same day he added this:

> O Sara, Sara, why am I not happy! why have I not an unencumbered Heart! these beloved Books still before me, this noble Room, the very centre to which a whole world of beauty converges, the deep reservoir into which all these streams and currents of lovely Forms flow – my own mind so populous, so active, so full of noble schemes, so capable of realising them – this heart so loving, so filled with noble affections....

He does not say as much but it must have deepened his depression when he compared his condition with that of Wordsworth, securely and happily married by this time, looked after by two devoted women, beginning his own family and writing better than ever.

Increasingly, Coleridge talked about leaving England to find a drier, healthier climate. He thought of Madeira, even India. There were sound health reasons for this, but he was also, once again, looking for escape.

By this time his brother-in-law Robert Southey had finally agreed to come and share Greta Hall with the Coleridges. Southey and his wife, shattered by the recent death of their only child, moved north in September 1803. Coleridge hoped that his wife might be cheered by her sister's company, and also, perhaps, that the presence of others in the house might diminish the danger of connubial quarrels. It did not work. Mrs Southey – and another sister, Mrs Lovell, who was also living there – joined the chorus of criticism against him. Just before Christmas, Coleridge left Keswick, virtually abandoning his family to Southey's care. In April 1804 he sailed for Malta, cutting himself off from both family and friends.

He was to live another 30 years. He was to live again in the Lake District – not with his family but as a guest of the Wordsworths in Grasmere – for months at a time. He was to explore the island of Malta and, on a visit to Sicily, climb the slopes of Mount Etna. But his departure from Keswick at the end of 1803 marked the effective end of his days as a fell-walker. The extent of his collapse is indicated in a description of Coleridge that Dorothy Wordsworth wrote in April 1810, when he was staying with them at Allan Bank: 'He lies in bed, always till after 12.o'clock, sometimes much later; and never walks out – Even the finest spring day does not tempt him to seek the fresh air; and this beautiful valley seems a blank to him'.

My post-circumcursion experience was, I am glad to say, nothing like that of Coleridge. I returned to my former Keswickian routine – researching and writing articles and books (including this one), playing tennis, reading and drinking, guiding visitors up the mountains.

It is all too easy, when you live in the Lake District, to take the place for granted and to forget the impact it makes when you come to it fresh, from elsewhere. Mountain guiding has saved me from that fate. The job makes me go out for a day-long walk, whatever the weather, two or three days each week. And it introduces me to scores of people, many of whom have never been to the District before. They often find the walking rather tougher than they expected but, almost unanimously, they also find themselves astonished and delighted by the experience. Most of them are on holiday from busy lives in the towns and cities. It is, for them, an introduction to a different world. They feel something of the revelatory joy that Coleridge felt when he first set eyes on the fells and told Dorothy Wordsworth, 'It was to me a vision of a fair Country'.

Coleridge founded no fell-walking 'school', had no immediate disciples. But gradually, as the century advanced, other men and women made the same discovery. The historian Basil Willey described the process in his book *Nineteenth Century Studies* (Chatto & Windus, 1949):

> ... I think that the whole course of English thought and letters in the nineteenth century would have been different if this island had not contained the mountain paradise of Westmorland and Cumberland. The Lake District was part of its religious creed .... The Alps, indeed, offered their rarer ecstasies to the leisured and the adventurous, but the Lakeland mountains, linking heaven with home, spoke more healingly and intimately to the heart.... Doubtless Wordsworth had much to do with this, but I suspect that even without him the clear streams, the exquisite grass and flowers, the bog-scented air, the silence and the solitude of the district would have supplied their tonic and anodyne to the townsmen and the inhabitants of Doubting Castle. For an England becoming steadily smokier and more hideous, and becoming less and less assured of its spiritual foundations and direction, it was (as it still is) of momentous importance that there should remain a region owing nothing to human contrivance and undesecrated by human hand, which could symbolise permanence, grandeur and joy ...

These are the qualities that Coleridge found. And, although it is no longer possible to describe the District as 'undesecrated by human hand', and though the tenor of modern thought tends to the secular rather than the spiritual, tens of thousands still come every year to follow his pioneering example and taste the exhilaration that he described.

Select Bibliography

I have used many printed sources in writing this book, naming them as I went along. For those who are particularly interested in the subject, it may be helpful to have a list of the more important books.

Key Sources
Collected Letters of S. T. Coleridge, edited by Earl Leslie Griggs, volumes 1 and 2, The Clarendon Press, Oxford, 1956.
The Notebooks of S. T. Coleridge, edited by Kathleen Coburn, volume 1, published for the Bollingen Foundation Inc. by Pantheon Books, New York, 1957.

Contemporary Sources
Budworth, Joseph, *A Fortnight's Ramble to the Lakes,* first published 1792.
De Quincey, Thomas, *Recollections of the Lakes and the Lake Poets* (essays first published in the 1830s, now collected in a Penguin edition).
Hazlitt, William, *My First Acquaintance with Poets,* 1823.
Hutchinson, William, *The History and Antiquities of Cumberland,* first published 1794.
Martineau, Harriet, *A Description of the English Lakes,* 1858.
West, Father Thomas, *A Guide to the Lakes,* first published 1778.
Wordsworth, Dorothy, *Journals,* edited by E. de Selincourt, Macmillan, 1941.
Wordsworth, William, *The Prelude,* the 1799 version.
A Guide through the District of the Lakes, first published 1810.

Modern Sources
Coburn, Kathleen, *In Pursuit of Coleridge,* Bodley Head, 1977.
Collingwood, W. G., *The Lake Counties,* first published by J. M.

Dent in 1902, revised by William Rollinson for the same publisher in 1988.

Gill, Stephen, *William Wordsworth: A Life,* The Clarendon Press, Oxford, 1989.

Holmes, Richard, *Coleridge: Early Visions,* Hodder and Stoughton, 1989.

Lefebure, Molly, *Samuel Taylor Coleridge: A Bondage of Opium,* Victor Gollancz, 1974.

Cumberland Heritage, Victor Gollancz, 1970 (this includes her essay on Coleridge, 'The First of the Fell Walkers').

Moorman, Mary, *William Wordsworth: A Biography,* Oxford University Press, 1957.

Nicholson, Norman, *The Lakes,* Robert Hale, 1977.

Greater Lakeland, Robert Hale, 1969.

Symonds, H. H., *Walking in the Lake District*, Alexander Maclehose, 1933.

Afforestation in the Lake District, J. M. Dent, 1936.

Index